THE EVOLUTION OF SKATING

LIVE, LOVE, SK8 TO TELL

VOLUME I

Amirah Palmer

Copyright ©2021, 2022, 2024 by Amirah Palmer
All rights reserved.
Printed in the United States of America

This book or any portion thereof may not be reproduced or used in any manner whatsoever without the express written permission of the publisher except for the use of brief quotations in a book review or scholarly journal.

Published by
SK8RZ Konnect
3695 Highway 6 South, Suite 114
Sugar Land, Texas 77478
eMail: publisher@sk8rzkonnect.com
Website: www.sk8rzkonnect.com

ISBN: 979-8-9865272-7-7 (paperback)

Library of Congress Control Number: 2022908124

Book Cover and Interior Design:
Jessica Tilles of TWASolutions.com

Special discounts are available on quantity purchases by corporations, associations, educators, and others. For details, contact the publisher.

All SK8RZ Konnect titles are distributed by:
Ingram Content
www.ingramcontent.com

Dedications

*After giving honor to Allah (swt)
and with heartfelt love and gratitude,
I dedicate this book to:*

My Brother

In appreciation of your unwavering love and support, even during times when my path was unclear. You've been a constant in my life, serving as my protector and everlasting best friend. Your resilience and determination have inspired me to strive for the best, and for that, I am eternally thankful.

My Son

Your presence has added a profound beauty to my life. From the very first moment I looked into your eyes, my heart has overflowed with enduring love and affection for you. Witnessing the man you've become fills me with immense pride. You are cherished unconditionally.

Acknowledgments

"Art is the silent expression of thoughts feelings and experiences."

~ Marilyn O

Roller skating transcends being merely a sport; it evolves into an art, a manifestation of personal expression on wheels. Each skater silently communicates the thoughts of their mind, the emotions of their heart, and the unique experiences they wish to share. It's not a skill learned; it's a sensation felt. While there exists a framework of style and rhythm, the individual's expression is distinctly their own.

No two skaters will provide an identical experience. Despite similar moves, the feelings inspiring those actions stem from their unique life journeys. This acknowledgment extends to a remarkable tribe of talented, skilled, educated, and dedicated individuals contributing to this project, both directly and indirectly. In the introspection of 2022, I realized that this book was my dream, and none of you initially signed up for this venture. Yet, collaboratively, we are crafting history, leaving behind a legacy to cherish, all to preserve and safeguard a beloved culture.

Special thanks to those who visually catalog our artistry: Linwood Neverson of Sk8Kingz Media, Doug Mike of Sk8 Vidzz, Terrance Glover of Triple 7 Magazine, Sk8CultureClub, Wes Jiggs, Jayson Vernon, Chad Harrell of SkateLyfe TV, Robert Dea, David Pippen of SkatePhotos.com, Roll Modul, Tyrone Dennis, Malik Thomas of Sk8 Chicago, Scotty Moson, Dr. L. David Stewart of Year60 Photography, Rogelio Valdez, Kurby Brown, Fabrice Bueno, Chuck Williams of

WBSA TV, Debra Chase of Timeless Connections, KappaChris Robinson, Short Shots, Larry Black, Timeless Connections, Glennesha Johnson of DWL Studios, Scott Rinaldi of Scott Rinaldi Photography, Above Ground Photography, Sk8Luv33, Nate Wren, Queen City Skate TV, Ron Fussnecker of Midwest Skaters and the many others who have contributed and are nameless, I thank you and send a wealth of gratitude to you all. Forgive me for those not mentioned. Charge it to my mind and not my heart.

    Peace and Blessings to all,

Amirah Palmer

Contents

Preface ix

Clyde McCoy, aka Ice From Philly 1

Dr. L. David Stewart, aka Nizm 7

Michelle Barrios 15

Darius Stroud, aka D-Breez 21

Paul Johnson 29

Ginger Mathews, aka Skate Critic 35

Michael Giles, aka Diddy 45

Lawrence Thomas/Michael Giles, aka Jit and Diddy 51

Richard Houston, aka Rockin Richard 55

Myesha McCaskill, aka Smooth Goddess 63

James Rich, aka BuckWild 67

Eric Alston 75

Chuck Burch, aka Chuck From Detroit 79

Lynna Davis, aka Lynna Moving Star 85

Tony Sailor, aka Sick On Skates 91

Doug Mike, aka Sk8 Vidzz 97

Berri Blanco, aka Strawberry Perez 101

Eugene White, aka Quad1 105
Featured Skater: Okurut George, aka B-Boy Skater George 111
In Memoriam and Tribute to Yanice Brinkley 115
Amirah Palmer, the Lead Author 119

Preface

"Out of every adversity, comes opportunity."

~ Benjamin Franklin

This quote resonates deeply, particularly in the context of the COVID-19 pandemic that forced a significant shift in our daily, work, and social lives. The virus's impact has been profound, rearranging life in unexpected ways. Whether through personal experiences with friends, family, or coworkers, we have all been touched by the pandemic's effects—ranging from early deaths, unemployment, to loneliness and financial instability.

The pandemic prompted a forced stillness, compelling individuals to sit, focus, and recalibrate their lives. It was a moment where the realization of not being in control became apparent. In the silence, people began to grow, reevaluate life from a different perspective, and face the choice of sinking or swimming. Financial struggles were intensified for those already on the brink, and health battles were waged with some facing lingering issues.

The same held true for me. During the pandemic, I hosted a podcast where skaters would visit my studio to share their experiences, history, and passion for roller skating. When quarantined, I had to shift and began conducting interviews via Zoom. As I adapted, a concern crept into my soul—what if this history, our history, is lost? How can I ensure our stories are preserved? Books have always stood the test of time, so I thought of writing a book, a logical choice. But where do I begin? Seeking guidance, I called Ice From Philly, seeking his advice and blessings on this journey. After thorough discussions, he saw the merit in this endeavor and agreed to assist, connecting me with individuals who could contribute to this meaningful project. To him, I am forever grateful.

I aim to take you on a journey into the heart of skate culture, unraveling the passion that fuels our love for the art and sport. This collaborative effort brings together members of the skate community, sharing their stories of introduction, acceptance, growth, and mastery in the artistry and skill of roller skating. I welcome you to immerse yourself in the passion of each contributor, gaining insight into the unique roles we all play in shaping this culture. The evolution of roller skating continues to unfold, offering a versatile experience that can be enjoyed alone or with family and friends. It stands as an inclusive activity, welcoming individuals regardless of race, religion, social, or financial status.

As you delve into each narrative, I encourage you to approach it with an open heart, engage your mind, connect with your soul, and embrace the unfolding journey—the crafty and innovative.

Peace and Blessings

Amirah Palmer

Clyde McCoy
aka Ice From Philly

Facebook: @Icefromphilly | Instagram: @icefromphilly

"I am not a skater, I am an artist! Artists are constantly creating."

Also known as Ice from Philly, I have been roller skating since the age of two, starting in Philadelphia, Pennsylvania, at the Saint Charles Borromeo Skating Rink. My passion for skating began at this age when my brother, Robert Horsey, one of the house deejays, would take me to the rink. Both my mother and brother were also skaters. I later started roller skating in the streets and developed a love for watching Roller Games/Roller Derby. Over the years, I honed my skills at various rinks across Philadelphia and in the Tri-state area, as well as in different rinks across the United States. During this time, I incorporated several dance disciplines, including tap dance, breakdance, ballet, jazz, modern, steppin'/hoofing, along with martial arts.

Simultaneously, I was a member of the South Philly Franchise Dancers, where I and several other dancers would watch and emulate moves from The Nicholas Brothers, The Berry Brothers, Fred Astaire, Gene Kelly, Soul Train Dancers, and many other dancers worldwide. Alongside fellow skaters Wayne Woodford, John Covington, Orlando Brown, Wayne Hanner, William Jones, and others, we attempted these moves while on roller skates.

In 1981-82, I encountered a group of guys, The Philadelphia Wizards on Wheels, who entered the Great Skate skating rink half an hour before closing and proceeded to shut it down with a performance lasting at least fifteen minutes.

Between 1982-1985, The Original Wizards on Wheels disbanded due to life events. During this period, I joined the group Rhythm on Wheels (1985-87) and met my skate partner Lisa Campolo-

Goodheart, Esquire. Over time, Lisa and I formed the duo High Energy, performing at several venues in the Tri-state area. We were featured in a story by the Philadelphia Daily News and on various Television and news shows. After appearing on the Television show Visions, we received numerous performance requests. It was at this point that I invited other top skaters in Philly, including two original founding members of the Wizards (Anthony "Tex" Smith and Wayne "Shorty" Grimes), to join me and Lisa. In 1987, Lisa and I combined our talents and embraced change, forming the 1987 version of The Philadelphia Wizards on Wheels.

From 1987 to 2007, the Wizards became a household name in Philly, performing at all of the city's top major events, including parades, cultural events, music venues, movies, tours, and performances with notables such as Kirk Franklin, Tom Joyner, Public Enemy, and many others. The Wizards received numerous awards and citations, including receiving the Key to the City.

I have been a professional performing roller skating artist for well over thirty years with several Philadelphia-based Roller Skating Performing Groups, including Rhythm on Wheels (1984-1986) and High Energy (1986-1987). I assisted performances with Wheels of Fire (1992-1994) and was the frontman with The Philadelphia Wizards on Wheels (1987-2014) and with several dance companies, as well as a Solo Artist from 2008 to the present, performing in over eleven different countries.

I have been a member of SAG/AFTRA since 1987 and have appeared in several motion pictures, including Luther's Choice, The Rocky Series, Philadelphia, the special feature section of Roll Bounce, Law Abiding Citizen, and Creed I and II, as an extra. Over the years, I have also been featured in several magazines, newspapers, and Television commercials. Additionally, I performed at several world-famous venues in the United States, including The Apollo, The Uptown, The Met, The Grand Old Opry, The Lincoln Center, Valley Forge Music Fair, Central Park, Venice Beach Skate Park, The Residence Rink, and for Mayors, Presidents, and a King from Africa at the Odunde Festival with the Wizards, in addition to President Obama's inauguration. I have also been blessed to perform overseas and with several famous celebrities, actors, musicians, and Broadway performers.

Several of my major highlights within skating include teaching an artistic child how to skate, working with the Special Olympics, and coming in second place in a talent show with the singing group Boyz II Men. The audience actually thought we won, but all the judges were from the recording industry.

I have helped and continue to assist many of my fellow roller skating artists, deejays, and other components within the skating industry in the United States and other countries over the years. I continue to seek wisdom and guidance from my elders worldwide while imparting such to the youth and embracing the evolution and change from the youth within the art.

Do You Know...

How Angular Moment is Used?

Angular momentum plays a crucial role in roller skating, particularly when executing spins or turns. Angular momentum is a measure of the rotational motion of an object around its axis. When a skater initiates a spin or turn, they manipulate their body's distribution of mass to control their rotational speed.

To understand this concept, consider a skater performing a spin. Initially, the skater's body possesses a certain amount of angular momentum. By bringing their arms closer to their body or extending them outward, the skater alters their distribution of mass. According to the conservation of angular momentum, as the skater adjusts their body position, the product of their moment of inertia (which is affected by the distribution of mass) and angular velocity remains constant. Therefore, when the skater decreases their moment of inertia by bringing their arms closer to their body, their angular velocity increases, resulting in a faster spin. Conversely, when the skater extends their arms outward, increasing their moment of inertia, their angular velocity decreases, slowing down the spin.

Similarly, when executing turns, skaters adjust their body position to control their rotational speed. By shifting their weight and positioning their limbs, skaters can modify their moment of inertia and thus their angular velocity. For instance, during a tight turn, skaters may tuck their body inward to decrease their moment of inertia, allowing for a faster rotation. Conversely, during a wide turn, extending their body outward increases their moment of inertia, resulting in a slower rotation.

In summary, skaters utilize angular momentum by manipulating their body's distribution of mass to control their rotational speed when executing spins or turns. Understanding this principle enables skaters to adjust their technique effectively, enhancing their ability to perform complex maneuvers with precision and grace.

Dr. David L. Stewart
aka Nizm

Facebook: @DrDavid Stewart | Instagram: @nizmlaverite

"A King's Origin and Doctor's Arrival."

I've been a skater for over thirty-two years and a JB skater for twenty-four years. I was blessed to be a member and founder of a JB skate crew known as Suicide Kings.

My small contributions to the community included being a writer and co-producer of the song "Skate Music," and serving as a consultant on the Emmy-nominated documentary United Skates, amongst other things.

What I wanted to cover now was my story.

I grew up on the South Side of Chicago. My mother was a skater, but my father was not. My parents raised me during a time when gang culture was prevalent in a different way. At the time, I thought skating was "not cool." I only saw figure skating and didn't think it was cool. Then one Saturday, I saw JB skating for the first time. They were fraternity brothers of my dad, and watching them skate to The J.B.'s song, "You Can Have Watergate, Just Gimme Some Bucks and I'll Be Straight," hypnotized me. I remember standing on the "little" floor at The Rink Fitness Factory (a.k.a. 87th). At that moment, I decided I wanted to know and learn that.

Then, I began taking lessons on Saturday mornings from a gentleman named Sam. I was also learning figure skating from a skater named Houston. I did all this while rolling on rental skates (a.k.a. potatoes). From 1989 to 1993, skating was my life.

After running into "trouble" in the neighborhood, my mother moved me to the opposite end of the city over Christmas break in 1993. The move was also important as it was a chance for me to be free of "troubles," however, it separated me from my friends at the Rink. So from 1993 to 1997, I did not skate at all!

The Evolution of Skating: Live. Love. Sk8 2 Tell: Volume I

Fate would have it in 1997, early in my senior year of high school. A friend asked me to come to a skating party at a rink known as Rainbo Roller Rink. This rink was on the north side of Chicago and more diverse, but I didn't go to it because I felt it wouldn't have the same vibe as The Rink. After being cajoled into going, I dusted off my old Dominions and said, "I 'used to skate,' so why not?" When I walked into that building that Saturday, I met people I would later call family and formed a crew, which I will talk about later. I saw these young skaters looking like me doing this style that I saw on the South Side but with their own flair to it. They weren't just skating to James Brown but hip-hop. For me, that was major because I was immersed in hip-hop as a graffiti artist and MC. So I got bit again by the bug to skate. At the end of senior year, when I wasn't out sharpening my skills as a battle rapper in Chicago under the moniker NIZM, I was out skating.

In 1999, a friend who I met through another friend and I got close. A Mexican gentleman who skated "like a brotha". We met because people both called us "stuck up" or conceited because we didn't talk, just skated. He and I then sized each other up as skaters, and then learned we both respected the other and we became good friends. To this day, we are like family, and I am the godfather of his daughters and his deranged dogs (LOL). Spicy, as he is known, and I began skating and learning JB routines. We then saw these two older gentlemen who embodied the cool and style we wanted. One was tall and quiet, but menacing. The other was shorter with a sharp sense of humor and quick to crack jokes, but they were no joke on skates. One Saturday, at a midnight ramble, we wanted to learn from them, and they ignored us! Dismissed us as if we didn't exist. We skated behind them, and they kept rearranging the sequences at will so that we could never learn them. This went on for over three months! They had this one move in the middle they would do that we would later learn as the "GaGa," which was originated from other JB skaters, a few generations prior, but at the end, they would do this collapse on their knees that gave visions of James Brown and it would shut down the crowd! We were irritated! We wanted to learn, but they wouldn't show us! So, we each assigned ourselves one of the two to observe and we were going to get it! One fateful Sunday they did their thing, and they concluded with their regular applause and awe from the crowd. They knew they were amazing. Spicy and I went out on the floor and mirrored them. We mimicked their moves to a tee! When we did their finale, we dropped down and looked back at them, with a quiet but serious bravado that without words stated "WE CAN DO IT, TOO!" From that moment, the informal forming of a crew was born.

In 2003, I was finishing my senior year of college at The University of Illinois-Chicago. March 3 was a day that would live in personal infamy for two reasons. One of which I will share here, one will be later. March 3, 2003, was the day that Rainbo Roller Rink closed. Capitulated to the political pressure from local politicians, it was a day of sadness. Like when many roller rinks close, everyone comes out to have a last memory to a place that meant so much to many of us. For many, it was the realization of going to "The Rink." For me, it was a homecoming. One fateful Sunday in the summer of 2003, we were in the middle of joking about what a crew name would be. A few of us debated, and we didn't want to put "JB" in front of it. So, we talked and from the conversation, we were like, what we do is suicidal. (If you see some of our moves, you would see why.) Then we were like, we are the king of the moves no one wants to try, and from that, Suicide Kings was born. Our founding date is March 3, 2003, officially, when Rainbo closed. If Rainbo never closed, this squad never formed, and some very famous people who are impactful to the skate world would not impact it today!

In 2004, a date that was once happy became my personal September 11 (aka personal tragedy). March 3, 2004, was the day my mother passed from a bout with lung and brain cancer. She was the reason I became a skater, and it created a void in me on so many levels. While in graduate school at the University of Toronto, I contemplated and, a few times, attempted suicide. I often walked around downtown Toronto at 3:00 a.m., listening to her favorite song, "Summer Madness" by Kool & the Gang on repeat. (When this song is on, I don't talk to people to this day). When I would come home, Spicy and the "Squad," aka "The Guys" (Suicide Kings), would encircle me and make sure no one would talk to me. Many times, I'd just roll. Skating in the place that makes you think of a lost parent is a lot. However, skating helped me to see better days.

From 2005 to 2012, skating gave me peace and clarity on what I wanted in life, who needed to be out of it, and career decisions. Concurrently, Suicide Kings, as a crew, had garnered a name on the local scene. We were those "tank top wearing $%^&." We skated in military formations, with matching outfits but with personalized elements (ex. black dress shirts, but different color ties), and when it was time to skate backward, we were infamous for stripping down to tank tops and performing erotically motivated moves on skates, that, well, ignited the imaginations and emotions of many a woman on a Sunday night. (Insert smirk here!)

Over time, as skating evolved, I went through more. Roughly from 2005 through 2009, I lost my grandmother, ended a tumultuous engagement, and relationship as being a very involved stepfather, and career setbacks while completing my first master's degree. Regardless of what was happening, skating was my "happy place." As I got older, I thought about the future of Suicide Kings, aka SK. I started thinking one day I wouldn't be here. Some of the older guys wouldn't be there. What would come of it? From there, the process of "Steinbrennering" (in honor of the late George Steinbrenner of the New York Yankees, who would look for talent to help the next generation and legacy of the organization) began. From that process, through our renowned rigorous "indoctrination process," we find diverse members who mesh with the group and continue to carry, strengthen, and uplift the brand and bond known as SK. For me, I learned about teaching, leadership, and how to be a mentor through Suicide Kings.

In 2016, the day for me to leave came. I moved to Miami, and the lessons would come full circle. While in Miami, I would begin the task of obtaining my Ph.D. while starting a new career. I would be leaving my first brotherhood (after forming SK I would go to become a member of Alpha Phi Alpha Fraternity, and a Freemason). However, from an informal group that started in 1999 to a group that now has eighteen members stationed all over the country, a king found his foundation to become a doctor.

2020, for many, was chaotic. The inception of the pandemic is self-explanatory. What further complicated 2020 for me was an ailing father. He had cirrhosis and liver cancer and had a stroke in May 2020. Skating was taken away because of the pandemic; there was no escape. He would pass in June 2020 and I couldn't skate. Our family couldn't have a proper service as only ten people could be present. Fighting depression, while finishing up a dissertation was the one thing that made me feel better. So, to combat that and weight gain, I began a variation of the keto diet to get back in shape. Irony would have it from that diet that I would be rushed to the hospital on November 20, 2020, with a blood sugar of 496 and sent to Cardiovascular ICU to prevent going into a diabetic coma. Waking up with needles in one's hands and insulin drips allow for moments of humble thought. After reaching out to close family and friends, I video called "The Squad." Their faces were of horror to see me in the hospital. I told them what was happening and made them swear to keep it quiet as I wanted to see the outcome of it. Their words gave me the courage to fight through it. Since that day I was diagnosed with Type-2 diabetes, but with skating, I got off of insulin shots in six months. While I currently still take some medication, no more shots, and soon to be done with the pills. Skating again was a big part of me coming back and getting my health together. My doctor was amazed at how well I regulated my blood sugar in such a short time. I told him prayer, eating, and skating.

After much chagrin, blood, sweat, and tears, I defended my dissertation on October 29, 2021, and became Dr. L. David Stewart. The journey was not without loss as I reminisce about my father, my mother, grandmother, and others lost along the way. However, through the foresight of my mother, I have skating and the brotherhood of the "World's Most Dangerous Skate Crew" Suicide Kings! A lot of people often associate me with the "leader" but that is the furthest from the truth. Our squad is a democracy and moves as a unit. No one man runs SK. These gentlemen taught and teach me daily. In our squad, we have cops, artists, financial analysts, dancers, DJs, producers, fathers, and grandfathers. All men of good repute. That when they lace up and get on wheels, showcase a passion individually and collectively compose a group, I proudly proclaim membership and call them my brothers. Without them, there is no Nizm.

As Dr. Stewart, I look forward to positively impacting the world through various avenues, including skating. But it is from this past and this history, I design my future to leave a ripple across the waters of time and make positive impacts for future generations to come. From suicidal thoughts to Suicide Kings, a king was made a doctor!

Did You Know...

About Jam Plugs?

Jam plugs serve as additional components that can be affixed to the toe stops of roller skate plates. Their primary function is to enhance the contact surface with the ground, thereby facilitating smoother and more stable maneuvers for skaters. By improving the stability and consistency of the contact point, jam plugs enable skaters to execute specific moves and tricks with greater precision and control, enhancing their overall performance and maneuverability on the roller rink or skating surface.

Michelle Barrios

Facebook: @Michelle Barrios | Instagram: @michelleptybcn

"The Birth of Skate Love Barcelona."

I've been a roller skater since my childhood. I'm originally from Panama, and I grew up skating at a rink called "El Patín Dorado" (The Golden Skate). I don't have images to document my happiness from that time, but I do have my diary from when I was eleven years old, where I wrote about my happiness from skating.

Unfortunately, the rink closed. After that, my skates were stolen, and I stopped skating and focused on my other passions. Apart from my career as a Graphic Designer, I was an advertising model, dancer, hostess, and singer in Panama. I decided to experience the world. Thus, in 1999, I moved to Madrid, Spain, and came back to skating. I never thought that I would come back to my childhood passion as an adult, and even more, to create something out of it.

After several visits to Barcelona and discovering the great vibes and surfaces of the city, I moved to Barcelona in 2006. One day, I found some quad skaters, and we immediately connected. They had the idea of organizing an outdoor party and invited me to join the team, which I did and started to help with graphics and promotion. After the project was over, I created my own brand to spread the roller dance vibes on Facebook as BCN Roller Dance. It started as a meetup community, where we started to organize small events, to dance for private shows or films (advertising/music videos), or to give classes.

There wasn't a roller dance movement in Barcelona around 2010-2012, so I started to post about other communities to show how cool this is and to grab attention. Mainly showcasing the outdoor movements from Central Park, NYC, Venice Beach, and London because we didn't have an indoor rink until recently.

I was always trying to bring this culture to Barcelona, creating interesting content to get new skaters to join us. In 2012, we were visited by thirteen international skaters. That visit was the start of the

International Roller Dance Jam in Barcelona that grew organically from 2012 to 2014, putting Barcelona in the spotlight of skate events.

After seeing the growth and rise in people's interest through the years, I felt it was time to make it a proper festival. I created the brand 'Skate Love Barcelona' in 2015. At that time, the festival promotions were part of BCN Roller Dance channels, but in 2018, I started to promote the festival on its own channels.

Starting 'Skate Love Barcelona' was extremely difficult. We started the festival with no infrastructure, money, or experience in this type of event to hold such a program. We didn't understand many things. We didn't have a "roller disco" culture here, and special venues that can be used to roller skate weren't all that helpful. As if this were not enough, some people who didn't understand or trust my vision decided to make things even more complicated by trying to sabotage the event.

Fortunately, the result of the first edition of 'Skate Love Barcelona' in 2015 was so magical that everyone was excited about the experience. It was a successful beginning and an emotional experience. The first edition of the festival was key to knowing and understanding what exactly we had. It helped us realize that there was a very open community willing to be part of our proposal.

The support received in the first edition surprised us. We did not have funds to cover the costs of our collaborators, but we were fortunate to have the support of many. Among them were the coaches, who came all the way from Australia to teach and share with the participants, to spread the love. One of the richest aspects of this event is the multicultural and intergenerational exchange.

From day one, strong ties were created, thanks to the affection of many collaborators. They bet on the festival with us, and likewise, we received honest feedback. This helped us perceive how our festival made a positive impact on many lives. My motivation is fueled by the amount of support that we have received throughout the four years of the festival, especially from those who contributed to the first edition offering their time, energy, talent, passion, and love to make it happen.

'Skate Love Barcelona' is an international music festival on skates, dedicated to a community that shares the passion for music, dancing, and rolling in a social and multicultural environment. Our mission is to grow and inspire the community, keeping the essence of our common passion with respect, love, and solidarity regardless of cultures, races, and genders. We want to help transform our world by delivering a distinctive festival while taking action to meet the SDGs—Sustainable Development Goals. Thus, we are very excited about this new commitment.

We are proud to currently meet several of these goals. According to the SDG's website, "The Sustainable Development Goals are the blueprint to achieve a better and more sustainable future for all. They address the global challenges we face, including poverty, inequality, climate change, environmental degradation, peace, and justice."

Skate Love Barcelona is a four-day event that happens in eight locations, being the biggest and most expensive production that includes indoor Skate Love Disco and an outdoor Beach Party. Both parties have to be created from scratch in empty spaces, putting the electricity, the lighting, bar, DJ table, and counting on the permission for the boardwalk closure.

We have a great program of eight indoor and outdoor activities. The activities include workshops in three different settings, the Barcelona city tour, Meet & Greet with the Biz, Networking for the skaters that want to promote their businesses, the Skate Love Disco, the Beach Party, and the Gastronomic Closure. And for this year's edition, we are working on introducing a new and exciting surprise activity. The workshops have been a crucial area of our festival due to the number of people interested in learning and improving their skills with great coaches from all over the world.

Skate Love has been growing organically year by year, and we keep doing our best to offer an amazing experience for the community. In 2021, we will be celebrating our fifth anniversary, seeing that we have already noticed a bigger interest than last year's event. Consequently, we are expecting around twelve hundred people from thirty countries at this year's edition.

Nine years ago, I started my skating projects with the mere intention of creating a local community where I can enjoy my passion for skating. I never imagined that it would become what it is today. Time puts everything in its place. If you keep the hard work, perseverance, and passion; if you take care of your project's essence and values, if you keep your eyes open to learning from your mistakes with humility, and most importantly if you keep the mental balance while working on your project, you can achieve amazing things.

Do You Know...

How Newton's Laws Affect Skating?

Newton's laws of motion are fundamental principles that govern the motion of objects, including those involved in roller skating. Roller skating adheres closely to these laws, particularly Newton's first law of motion, which states that an object will remain at rest or in uniform motion unless acted upon by an external force. In roller skating, this law of inertia is evident in the skater's continuous motion unless acted upon by forces such as friction or applied force from the skater's muscles.

The second law of motion relates force to an object's mass and acceleration. In roller skating, skaters utilize muscle force to propel themselves forward. The force exerted by the skater's muscles is directly proportional to the acceleration achieved, allowing skaters to increase or decrease their speed by applying varying amounts of force. Additionally, changes in velocity, such as speeding up, slowing down, or changing direction, involve the application of force in accordance with Newton's second law.

Furthermore, Newton's third law of motion states that for every action, there is an equal and opposite reaction. In roller skating, this law is exemplified when skaters push against the ground with their wheels. The ground exerts an equal and opposite reaction force, propelling the skater forward. Similarly, when a skater executes maneuvers like turns or jumps, they exert force against the skating surface, and the surface pushes back with an equal force in the opposite direction, enabling the skater to perform the desired action.

Overall, understanding and applying Newton's laws of motion are essential for skaters to effectively control their movements, accelerate, decelerate, and execute maneuvers with precision and efficiency while roller skating.

Darius Stroud

Facebook: @D-breez Darius | Instagram: @dbreez_darius

"From Mr. JB to Mr. IR"

I am fortunate that skating is generational in my family; both my mother and father skated. My sister also skated. My nieces and nephews skate as well. My father had trophies lined up against the wall from his participation in skating contests and was a competitive skater. My mother was a smooth jazzy skater. Skating is something I was born with. I wish others could understand that having a competitive nature is a good thing. It propels us to be better. The people I competed with helped me become as good as I was. They constantly pushed me to be better so that I could receive the smiles and applause in the rink.

At our local rink, some great skaters were legendary, and they used to meet up in the middle, or as we say, "crazy legging in the middle."

When I came up, there would be a group of legends including Poochie, Milt, Nate, and others. These guys were legendary, and they welcomed everyone. They never gave other skaters the stank face, shunned anyone, or came out to obliterate one's move when one came in the middle. Rather, they would applaud, correct, and encourage others, even showing them a move or two.

Back in the day, when I used to see skaters trying to do my moves, if we were cool, I would assist them on how to get the move correct. This was one of the remarkable things about skating with the older generation (OG's). But there is also the other side to that gentleness; there will be people who don't like you. Either way, it works out for the good.

My rivals would push and inspire me, so I couldn't stop being creative with my moves. As they learned my moves, I knew I had to come out with other moves to stay on top. All rivals became fuel for my fire.

A fun fact about me: I'm a gamer. My main game of choice is Grand Theft Auto 5. For the last seven to eight years, it has been unbelievable. My other games are NBA2K basketball, Call of Duty War Zone, Gran Turismo racing, and Assassin's Creed. There are a lot of skaters that are Gamers.

Gaming is another way to stay connected. The gaming world was our first experience with social distancing. It's a way for people from all over the world to connect without being physically together. The competitiveness in some of the games, for me, is equivalent to skating.

A humble understanding comes with growing older. With age, you begin to reflect on those who assisted you to get to your current level. We all learn things from others. The difference with skating is that when you come into it, you see something intriguing, and you want to learn it. You begin to learn directly from someone you know and tend to skate like them. A learner tries to mimic the teacher, but one must learn the move and add creativity to the move.

The Chicago-based JB style, which is a beautiful style, is now the dominating style nationwide. You must learn the foundation of the style whenever you want to start using it. Then, as you advance, you will begin to put your own creative twist on it.

I would be a bad instructor because I am the type of person that would have a hard time teaching you from the beginning if you want to learn a skate move. I lack the patience. Nonetheless, when you get your balance or reach a certain level, I can help you to understand what you are missing and guide you to perfect the move. I didn't learn directly from a lot of people. My personal style of learning is to watch a person and then apply my own creativity to it. There were a few people throughout the years that I did ask directly. I watched others and applied their methods as well.

This method allowed my mind to see their moves, break it down, and then figure out how it works with my body. I advise newcomers to try this method of learning.

The Nutcracker, a signature move that I was known for, made a lot of people think I studied this move and perfected it, but that's not how it happened. People from my old neighborhood and school knew that I used to dance. I liked Break Dancing, Michael Jackson, James Brown, MC Hammer, and the likes. Through dancing, I was able to do the splits. While dancing, someone would always challenge or battle me. At one dance event, someone challenged me, and I wanted to win. I decided I would drop into a split and come up immediately. I did just that. With the adrenaline pumping in my veins, I knew I had nailed it. It was like I won the Championship.

I brought the move to skating. I had seen someone in the Michael Jackson video do this move on skates. When my guys challenged me, I thought, "What the hell! I'm going to try this move."

I had never attempted this move on skates in the past, but like clockwork, I dropped it and pulled it back up with the shoulder wave. It was crazy. The crowd went wild. It goes back to my competitive nature, and I knew I nailed it yet again.

Then, on another date, a DJ mentioned how they used to jump five feet in the air and land in the splits. So, I pictured it in my mind, did that too, and nailed it.

Regarding being a GOAT (Greatest of All Times), of skating, can anyone ever master all the skate styles? I don't think so. No one is going to be great in every area. It's not about being a master of all styles but mastering yours. If you are on a stage with other masters of their style, who's going to shine the brightest? That's when you become a GOAT. I've witnessed people, whom you know are good, shy away from a contest. Some feel the spotlight is too bright and that's not what they are made for. Off the stage, that person is amazing, but on the stage, they crack under the pressure, whereas someone else can perform under pressure.

A GOAT is not the best skater of the year. They are the best skater of an Era. You have to put in a body of work as a great skater in your area. When you are that good as a skater, you change the atmosphere around you. When others want to skate like that person and learn from that person, that is the GOAT.

Skating is a hobby that we all do and enjoy. But as a GOAT, you're able to do something that people with boatloads of money, with powerful jobs cannot always do; something that they, in some instances, may never be able to do. You are creating something that can impact their lives and create a change within people. I also give accolades to people when their props are due. Even back in the day, I did this. It's humbled respect. You have to respect a craft you love before you can be great. You must be able to see greatness and appreciate greatness in others.

When you accomplish something that you set out to do, there is a euphoric moment. But what comes after that? Now that you have achieved being the best in your rink, what's next? Now, you must experience a few losses to appreciate your accomplishments. You must also understand what accomplishment is. When people congratulate you on a win, how do you respond? People want to be great, but don't know what comes with that. When you are labeled 'great', half of the skate world will love you and half of them will hate you, can you handle that? Then, you will try and remain that guy/girl for five, ten, or twenty years. It's lonely at the top, especially if you are not a people person.

For you to accomplish anything and remain on top, you must have people around you that can remind you why you are doing this. If no one congratulates you, what does it mean? The difference between the people on top and those who stay at the top is like those who are one-hit wonders in the music world.

When you are the champ or on top, you are elated. You have people coming at you from different directions for all the wrong reasons. You have no guidance because it's new and now you have to do something on this level or better to remain relevant. Those people tend to break under the pressure, they drug out, fall out, or they quit because most don't surround themselves with people who will challenge them, and tell them when they are wrong. If you are doing it for yourself, you must have some type of self-gratification that allows you to say, 'I'm cool'; otherwise, you end up being the best skater but you're hollow inside.

What you thought the win would fill within, you never get. You feel empty and lonely despite being the best. Now, you're looking at everyone else and feeling you have no meaning. It's like not being human because you have no emotion. That is the result of being lonely at the top and not knowing what to do next.

One thing I love and have always loved about skating is that you can do it alone and you can do it everywhere. You can also excel and be a star in your own right. My whole JB elite skate team were skaters who showed a higher level of skating. I had to respect not only their level of skating but their differences. People always seem to think a skate group must skate alike. Not my group. As good as I was, my friend, Tito, would have destroyed me in a crazy leg circle, and I knew it. When there would be a challenge in the middle, I would send Tito in the middle to destroy them. As a leader, I was able to identify and respect each of our team member's strengths and weaknesses.

Once national skate parties started to take off, Tito and I started to travel the country, not to lay down the law, but to experience the world with this skating stuff. You should travel the world so that you can appreciate your city. You can skate and do what you love to do everywhere now.

When we travel, the driver gets to choose the music. When I drive, many would assume my music of choice would be rap or hip hop, but I listen to a wide range of music. Most of the songs I listen to are aggressive like DMX's "What's My Name," or club bangers like Lil Jon & Bone Crusher's "I Ain't Never Scared," or strong thought-provoking like TI's "Still I stand," or pain-filled like Bon Jovi's "Wanted," and more. A lot of the music I listen to puts you in the mood or mindset to conquer something or to meet a challenge. I can also flip it to laid back music like Rick Ross' "Aston Martin Music." I love "In the Air Tonight" by Phil Collins. You have to be diverse musically. I used to Break Dance to Herbie Hancock "Rock It." We used to throw a piece of cardboard on the ground and go to work. Music is beautiful.

These days, JB music is progressive. Back in the days, we had three tempos—real slow like "Watermelon Man," mid-tempo like "Watergate," and then the high tempo like "Make it Funky" and "Cornbread." These days, DJ's are stuck on the high tempo; I wish we could go back to at least two tempos.

The thing I love about National and International parties like Independence Roll (IR) and other current skate events is that they are multi-racial and religious, everyone is welcome. We get more appreciation to see a variety of people from all over the world, to see all the varied skate styles and cultures. Once you start to travel and begin to see the world, you begin to appreciate the differences. It really opens your eyes to life. Let skating be your excuse to travel the world. Seeing the world allows you to appreciate your style even more. Before national skate parties and my travels, I didn't know if I even wanted friends outside of Chicago, but after experiencing travel, I was open to communicating with others all over the country. When you see other people from other countries attending these events and know that you and a total stranger actually love one another because of skating, you are experiencing something beautiful.

I built Independence Roll on music that touches people around the world. I choose DJs for the event that will touch all styles and cultures. When I began to travel nationally, the only time we would get to hear our music (JB) was during roll call and we used to show out when we were called to the skate floor. While I understood it, I didn't agree with it. We (JB skaters) would only get the last five or ten minutes of the night to skate to our music, outside of the roll call. It was sad. Now, you can hear JB music everywhere. It has been an adjustment for the DJ's and skaters. Over time, people have gotten used to skating to the music. Many are not even skating the JB style to the music, which is beautiful. Now, more producers are bringing the style to the music as well.

When we put IR together and I was choosing the DJs, DJ DMC was a no-brainer. He has been on board since day one and will be with me until he wants to stop.

DJ Joe Bowen also came on board in the beginning as he began gaining listeners from other states and is still rocking with me. Then, I went to get DJ Narcissistic from Ohio because he was making great noise in his area. Moreover, I wanted to let people know that IR wasn't just a JB party, that it was a national party and we would play all styles of music. Mz DJ Tone was our first female DJ, who was making noise outside of our city, and I felt like I could help. DJ Fly Ty and I had met inside Branch Brook Park skating rink in NJ a few years earlier. I liked his approach to learning JB music.

DJ Lil Brian is like a nephew. I helped him connect with a few event coordinators when he was a youngster on the scene. DJ CJ was the next phase of our up-and-coming DJ talents in our style. DJ Arson drove to the first IR after spinning at an event Friday night and brought other skaters with him. I admired that.

All the DJs are people I know, who are handling music on a national level, not just a local level. I also paired them up on various nights so that they can represent everyone, making it easier to convince others of our vision. I have also created a platform for new DJs to get introduced on a national level. In the last couple of years, I have been allowing young DJs to get a feature spot, giving them exposure as it is hard for a new DJ to get exposure on a national level.

Paul Johnson

Facebook: @Paul Antonio Johnson | Instagram: @langstoncjsiriyaxylanolan

"The South Got Something to Skate"

It all began one Friday night at Sparkles skating rink in Riverdale. Doug, the reason I even started skating, had been persistently asking me and my buddy, Dean, whom I've known since I was nine, about skating at the rink. We constantly resisted, even making biased comments about skating.

Doug wouldn't take 'no' for an answer. So, he essentially bet his entire allowance to cover whatever we wanted that Friday night. All he needed was to physically show us his vision. Eventually, Dean and I relented. We didn't even make it past the DJ booth before Doug was surrounded by pretty girls, greeting and hugging him. Dean and I exchanged a look like, *damn*.

We hadn't even expected there to be attractive people at the rink like that. Doug then took us to the Pro Shop and rented us our speed skates. They looked cool compared to the brownies, or should I say rental skates. He advised us to hold off on putting them on as they were playing some dance music. Afterward, we headed to the corner to dance with some ladies before lacing up. In fact, I hadn't even spent half an hour in the rink, and I was already sold on going again because I had ladies and popularity in the blink of an eye.

Doug said, "Get ready to skate because after the slow set, they gonna play our music."

We were like, "Wait! We have music?"

The slow set ended and 'chief rocka' started playing, and Doug started going crazy.

We exclaimed, "Let's go."

Mind you, we couldn't do a damn thing but roll and try not to fall. Meanwhile, Doug was doing all types of tricks, including a cross slide or, as the ATL OGs called it, the stab. Dean and I were sold. We said, "We gotta learn this."

I went home and rearranged my schedule around Friday nights. We started practicing weekly. No week off. No month off. After about a year and a half, the manager of the rink called us to his office and told us he would allow us to start skating on Sunday Adult night if we didn't fight, respected our elders, and didn't curse.

We said, "Okay, we're in."

By this time, I was the skate guard at SkateTowne, and Dean was the DJ. So, we never had to work at our rink on Friday or Sunday nights. Instead, we practiced on Fridays at Sparkles and Saturday nights at SkateTowne while on the clock.

Finally, the first Sunday came and we went. It was scary and super packed. Nonetheless, we skated well. The catch was that there were like seven to ten other skate crews, with names, chants, and popularity. We were some kids from the ghetto who weren't supposed to be there, but we held our own. We were getting outshone by the superior group (Vaughn's Crew). I had known him all these years and never knew the name of their crew. All I knew was when the blonde high-top fade was coming, you better get out of the way. There were other crews too. We made up names for them because we didn't know their names and didn't care.

We had one job: to be the best! We taunted and made fun of other crews but also worked hard to avoid looking like any of them. Our moves were super hard to replicate. Some of the crews didn't take kindly to us, and a lot of skaters complained to management that we were too young to be there, but we were backed by management. They couldn't do anything about it.

We started getting really good and climbed the ranks on our way to the top. We also faced a lot of tough times and met haters along the way. They still try to hate on DA ONES, but we reign Supreme.

I remember one night we were on our way home from the rink and stopped at a red light only to have a rival skate crew pull up on us and draw a gun on us. I stared down the barrel of a gun and didn't flinch. It's funny that years later I saw the guy who pulled a gun out on me. He said, "Hey, man! We wanted to scare y'all away from the rink. I wasn't gonna shoot y'all."

I also want to give a shout out to the Gorilla Brothers, with whom we always go into the game, alongside the Jungle Brothers, my Philly strut crew (Pops, Unk, Mike, the twins, and the whole family), Courtney and Ivan's crew, Kojak and Tee, Kelvin and Jamar (The Warriors), Ga.

Rampage, S.O.S, ATL squad, and last but not least, Vaughns' crew. You all pushed us to raise the bar in this ATL skate style world.

On our way to the top, we also had a special skate night with Destiny's Child. Me, Doug, Dean, and Titus were at the rink one Sunday night when we came across a group of four beautiful women. It was a match made in heaven. Every member of the crew except Doug kept trying to match me up with Latoya Luckett, who was taller than I was. I was barely six ft tall. He was six foot three. However, I approached another lady, that I had my eyes on from the start and asked her if I could skate with her. She looked at me like she wasn't coming unless her friends had someone to skate with. On cue, Dean, Doug, and Titus chose one of the girls.

Dean grabbed Kelly, Doug grabbed Latoya, and Titus grabbed the chocolate girl (I never knew her name). We all got to skate with them, showed out, and got to skate with them again. When the slow set came back, it was one of the best skate sessions I had. There was no drama from rival crews and no falls. We were flawless on the routines, and each of us had a lady to skate with all night. When it was time to go, we all went over to them to exchange numbers. Here, I got one piece of paper I wish I had saved because it had my partner's phone number and name. She wrote her name on the paper. It read: Bianca.

I said, "Okay, Bianca. I'ma call you."

She said, "That's not my name."

Then, she took the paper and wrote: BE-YON-CE. She told me they were staying at a hotel and we could come to hang out with them while they were here meeting with Jermaine Dupri and LaFace Records, that they were a singing group named Destiny's Child.

Later, I was trying to convince my crew that we should go hang out with them, even though we had school in the morning. We didn't go and the rest is history. They became famous. Two years later, the limo driver saw us at the rink and proceeded to tell me that they talked about us all night and on the way back to Houston.

Years later, Black people started owning skating rinks. Four were Black-owned and still are today: SkateTowne, Skate Zone, Metro Fun Center, and the most famous one, Cascade, which wasn't all that popular until the movie came out.

One Sunday, we were at Cascade, and a heavyset guy with dreads came into the rink, walked around, and sat in the corner. He watched us for three hours even as we enjoyed the whole Cascade vibe. It was a nice crowd, with a few crew members, but never like Sparkles. By this time, we were the top dogs of the rink, and we are still the top dogs because if my whole group comes to the rink, you all know what time it is.

Anyway, one Tuesday, we got a call saying we needed to come up to Cascade on Wednesday morning to shoot a commercial. We were like, "Okay!"

When we got there, we met the guy from Sunday, who said, "Y'all were killing that shit on Sunday."

And he wanted to know if he could get that same energy from us that Wednesday.

We said, "Hell yeah!"

The rest is history. Major blessings and shout outs to Chris Robinson for believing in us. He even referred us to Benny Boom for Ciara's "One, Two Step" video, which was a blast from the past because we already knew Ciara from when she used to dance at Sparkles. She grew up in the same area as us, just a little younger though.

All ATL's finest were there: 112, Killa Mike, Shawty Shawty. These were folks we knew from around the way. It made the video extra fun, clowning around with folks we grew up with. The iPod commercial was dope. We met Hi Hat (Missy Elliott's choreographer) and she saw us skate but didn't know we could dance. We had them hyped up.

Even down to the movie, where we had to teach TI and other actors how to skate the ATL style (Meagan Good owes me a cake too…). In the twenty-eight years that DA ONES have been a group, the original three members have clocked $750,000 and counting. If you add DJ Slim (Brandon), it's over eight hundred thousand dollars. Who knew a seventy-five dollar pair of skates could have a return profit of two hundred fifty thousand dollars? Even though we did all these things with skating, we were still humble. I am teaching the second wave of DA ONES as we try to return to the big screen.

The quote I live by is "Skating saved my life!" I hope skating saves a lot more lives along the way.

Growing up in College Park isn't a joke. So much could have happened but didn't because I was skating. Nowadays, as a skate pioneer and O.G. in the skate world, I love to educate skaters especially the new ones, who want to do the moves but don't want to pay homage. I see Facebook and Instagram posts all the time asking, "Who are the top five skaters?" I always comment, "ME." If you are talking top five groups, DA ONES is number one, hands down, and will probably be that way until I leave this earth.

Ginger Mathews
aka Skate Critic

Facebook: @Ginger Dawn Mathews | Instagram: @theskatecritic

"Birth of the Skate Critic"

I am known in the skate world as the Skate Critic. I travel around the world and review roller rinks. I post these reviews on several social media sites. I also keep track of all the live rinks, as well as the dead rinks in the United States. I am a freestyle/rex skater in the adult skate world. I come from a long line of skaters from many different avenues of the skate world.

My journey began before I was born. My maternal grandmother was an ice skater. My mother was an artistic roller skater and my father was a "Rink Rat." My father would go down to Valle Vista Skating Center in Hayward, California, on Friday and Saturday nights, trying to talk to my mother.

One day she told him, "If you're trying to get me to go out with you, you're going to have to learn how to skate."

He left and told Uncle Joe that he was done with that broad and didn't care if he ever saw her again. The following Friday, he returned with his entire paycheck and bought a pair of skates and learned how to skate. My mom passed away at twenty years old when I was only twenty-two months old. She never got to take me roller skating.

My father married my second mom, who was also an artistic roller skater. She told me that I was born to skate. Later, my second mom took me skating for the first time when I was four years old. I had a lesson not long after that at Valle Vista Skating Center in Hayward, California. I was in the center of the Skate Floor, having my lesson while the Saturday afternoon session was happening around me. I was not paying attention and goofing off.

Every once in a while my second mom would come out of nowhere skating by me at a hundred miles an hour, smacking my head and

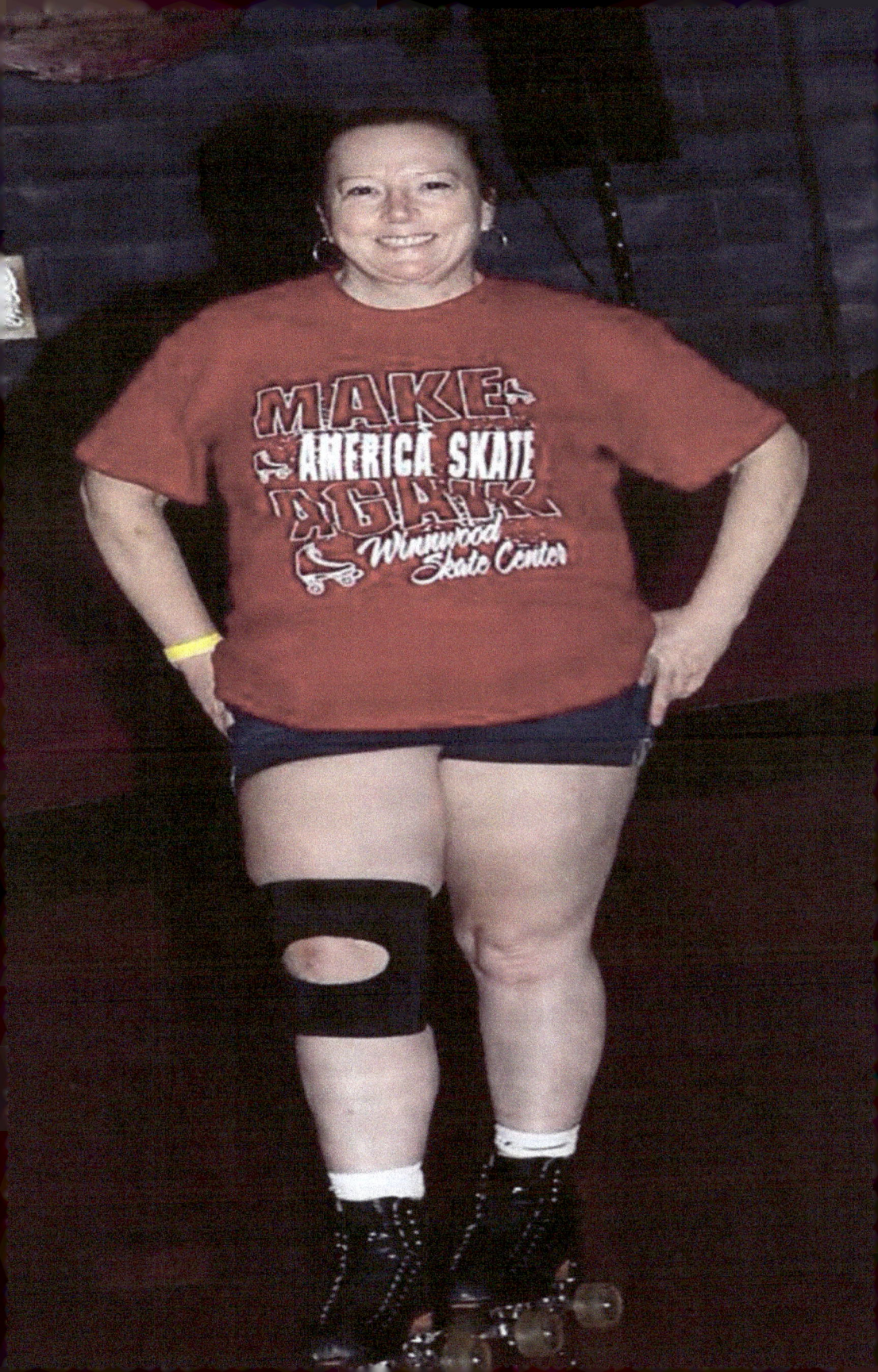

telling me to pay attention, then skate away as fast as she arrived. All I could think was, *Wow! I want to skate fast as she does.* Eventually, I was able to skate faster than her.

My father passed away when I was six, so my grandparents raised me. They would drop me off at Valle Vista Skating Center every weekend. I became a Rink Rat like my father. When I was around nine or ten, I went to my aunt's house for the summer in Roseville, California. She took me to her rink, Roller King.

I remember walking in and thinking, *What's wrong with this rink? Why is the floor blue?* I was totally fascinated with everything different about this rink. From then on, I wanted to see inside every rink. I wanted to see what was different. My grandparents rarely obliged.

When I was sixteen, I would pick up my friend Cyndi from BART (Bay Area Rapid Transportation) because she didn't drive to go to Valle Vista Skating Center.

One day she said, "You have a license and a car."

I replied, "Yeah…"

She said, "We can go to any rink we want."

I said, "Yes!"

Away we went, going to other rinks, increasing my fascination.

I got married a few times, had kids, and vowed that I would not make my kids skate orphans until they could get into the adult skates. I planned all our vacations around visiting at least one rink each year. Finally, my youngest son was able to petition his way into the adult skate at San Jose Skate in San Jose, California, at the age of fifteen. It was game on from there.

I come from a long line of skaters as I stated earlier. My uncle was a pro. My aunt and uncle are artistic roller skaters, roller derby, and roller hockey skaters. They also played on the Bay City Bombers and owned a rink called Roller Faire in Pleasanton, California. My family has their hands in three Roller Derby teams in the Central Valley of California, and my uncle wrote the rules for Flat Track Derby. One of my cousins was also on the Bay City Bombers, coached roller derby, played roller derby, and roller hockey. Another cousin played roller hockey and was on the USA team that won Gold. Both of their spouses are skaters too. Like I said earlier, my mom and second mom were artistic roller skaters. Grandma was an ice skater and my father was a Rink Rat. I almost forgot, my uncle/godfather was also an artistic roller skater. My grandfather worked at a traveling Roller Rink in the 1930s in Texas, and then there's me.

I went in a totally different direction from the rest of my family. I became an adult skater, following the adult circuit skate parties around the United States. During my travels, I would hit as many rinks as I could. Each trip, I'd usually hit an average of ten roller rinks plus the skate party and a few adult skate sessions.

My first goal was to skate at every rink in California. While accomplishing this goal, my family would often tell me, "You need to write this down. You need to take pictures. People want to know."

I would just fluff them off and say, "Yeah! Yeah! Yeah!"

Soon skaters began asking me about rinks because I had been to so many. Then, I went to a roller derby game and my aunt said to me again, "You need to write this down. You need to take pictures. People want to know."

I said to her, "Yeah! Yeah! I'll be the Skate Critic."

Lord, I had no idea what was about to happen. I completed my California goal and then a new roller rink opened in Murrieta, California.

I headed to the Los Angeles area on New Year's Eve 2013 to reclaim my title. I was going to the new roller rink Epic Rollertainment in Murrieta, California on New Year's Day, 2014. I thought that I would just skate at one of my other favorite roller rinks in the Los Angeles area for New Year's Eve with my friends.

But no! All the Los Angeles rinks were fifteen and under lockdown, meaning that unless you had a kid with you, you weren't going! Ugh! Here I was in my Hotel Room, bored. I thought, let me check into this Skate Critic thing. I searched everywhere, and no one was doing any kind of rink reviews.

I went on Facebook, Instagram, Twitter, Tumbler and YouTube. I started my group "Skate Critic" with thirty-three friends in it. All night my phone would not shut up. By the next day, there were over eight hundred people in my Skate Critic group on Facebook.

When I returned from this trip and went to my local adult skate at Golden Skate in San Ramon, California, all my friends asked me, "What did you do?" I said, "I don't know but we're rolling with it" No Pun intended. And then, the Skate Critic was born.

Today, Skate Critic has over 6,400 members. I have over 10,000 followers behind the scenes and I'm just amazed. Of course, I can't stop there.

I was absolutely annoyed with all the rink lists online. They were outdated by over seven years at that point. Today, those lists are outdated by over thirteen years. I would go to addresses listed for rinks and find empty lots. Some of them had been vacant for close to ten years.

I set out to fix this problem. I downloaded every rink list and made a huge master list. Then, I proceeded to call every rink to verify that they were still in business. I hired some friends and family and we started calling. Numbers were disconnected, businesses had closed, burned down, moved, or changed area codes.

Every time, we ran into an error, we had to investigate it further to find out if the rink really was gone, the area code was changed, they changed buildings, changed names, changed owners, or if they were burnt to the ground? After eighteen months, I had a working live rink list.

It was and still is better than any list out there! Yes! No more driving to a rink to find out they were gone. The byproduct of this project was a dead rink list, which was to make sure that roller rinks are not forgotten.

As of today, my dead rink list is up to 9,978 rinks in the United States. I suspect there are at least 2,000 more rinks I have not uncovered yet. The live rink list is one of my greatest accomplishments.

Every other year, I call all of these rinks to make sure they are still in business and constantly monitor the Internet to research roller rinks. My following is so massive that people notify me of rinks opening and closing all the time.

As of today, the live rink list is at 1,244 rinks in the United States and about seventy in the rest of the World. Many rinks have fallen during the pandemic. I will not know the extent of this damage until after it is over.

Then I can call all the rinks to see which ones made it.

Of course, my lists don't stop there! Why should they? I have the most up-to-date lists for:
- For Sale Roller Rink
- Adult Skate Roller Rink
- Adult Skate Party
- Roller Rink Owners
- Adult Skate Music
- Black-owned Roller Rink
- Future Roller Rink Owners
- Master Roller Rink
- Ages of the Rink itself
- Regular Rink Rules
- Adult Skate Rink Rules
- Rotunda Floor
- Top Twenty-Eight Oldest Roller Rinks
- Top Ten Largest Skate Floors
- Top Twenty Largest Skate Floors
- Top Ten Smallest Skate Floors

I'm sure there are a few more I've forgotten.

What happens next? As I was traveling along through the skate world, reviewing roller rinks, I was approached at a skate party at Roller Dome in Richmond, Virginia, to be part of a skating documentary. I said, "Sure, but you're going to have to call me because I gotta go skate."

If anyone knows me, when I'm at a Skate Party, I'm the first one on the skate floor and usually the last one off. I skate fast and hard all night. Well, they did call me for five years as we worked on this documentary. Of course, most of my work was behind the scenes checking facts. I made an appearance five times in the film with one part of a line I always say when talking about the sad fate of our roller rinks in the United States.

"On average, we lose three rinks a month in the United States. You may get one that re-opens and maybe a new one."

There is a scene in the *United Skates Documentary* of the United States map with the locations of nearly 5,000 roller rinks we had at one time. The clock rolled forward and the roller rinks went away until we were left with 1,256 roller rinks at the end of production. This scene was all my work brought to life on the big screen. Everywhere it was shown, it brought the entire audience to tears or gasps.

I cried at the premiere when I saw it and heard the audience. Finally, people were grasping what I was seeing every day. I have reviewed and skated at 398 roller rinks as of today. My current goal is to surpass Sure-Grip Steve who has visited 460 rinks. Once I achieve this goal, I can enter the *Guinness Book of World Records*. Then, I can say I have skated at the most roller rinks in the world.

Of course, I won't stop there! My other goal is to say I've skated at every roller rink in the world.

You're probably asking about my reviews. When I walk into a rink, I look at their floor, employees, snack bar, bathrooms, and DJ. All rinks are graded by wheels, one through eight. Example: Eight Wheels means perfect and any less than that means you have some things to work on. Eight Wwheels also means you have a full set of wheels to skate on. I give out Toe Stops to rinks that are over the top after they've achieved Eight Wheels first! To date, there are only two rinks with Eight Wheels and Two Toe Stops. Those rinks are Oaks Park Roller Rink in Portland, Oregon, also known as The Oaks, and Semoran Skate Way in Casselberry, Florida. After I am done looking for my criteria and measuring the skate floor, I then start looking at what makes this rink special from other rinks. I try to capture the uniqueness of the rink in photos and videos. When I am finished with that, I look for the owner or the manager to find out some facts about the rink. What year was it built? Who originally started it? Who owns it now? Do you have an Adult Night? Does your rink still have the old school stickers or patches? Tell me some history about the rink and any other questions I come up with while rolling at their rink. Then, I'll point out the problems I found in the rink and see when they are going to be addressed.

About a week after I leave, I'll finish their review and post it to Facebook, Instagram, and Twitter. Then, I'll post any of the videos on

YouTube. I also catalog and save everything in case something happens to that roller rink, so we have it for historical value or insurance if necessary.

I have been featured on YouTube, radio stations, podcasts, movies, videos, magazines, newspaper articles, TV news and at the Roller Skating Association's Convention. You can find me in attendance at various roller skating events throughout the country such as Roller Derby, Speed Skating, Artistic, Skate parties, Adult Skates, Regular Sessions, Skate fundraisers, RSA Conventions, USARS, also known as USA Roller Sports and many others.

If you see me at your local roller rink measuring the skate floor, I invite you to say, "Hi." If you dare, join me on a skate trip. See if you can hang out with the Skate Critic. I generally wear people out. They usually quit the first day and opt to stay at the hotel for the rest of the trip. I've only had a few people go to more than one rink with me on a trip. There's only one person that has been able to hang every day on several trips.

I also sell Roller Skates for Golden Horse Roller Skates, the artistic line out of our local rink Paradise Skate in Antioch, California which is under the brand Paradiseskatewholesale.com. I am sponsored by Susan Geary of RollerSkater.com and always looking for more opportunities in the skate world to pay for my "hobby that's lost its mind!"

In closing, ask yourself what you can do to make the roller skating world a better place. Be yourself and watch what grows. You never know what you will become accidentally.

Do You Know...

That Roller Skating Involves Physics?

Roller skating encompasses a fascinating array of principles from physics, biomechanics, and engineering, making it a captivating blend of science and sport. From a physics perspective, the motion of a skater involves concepts such as Newton's laws of motion, friction, and momentum. The way skaters accelerate, decelerate, and maneuver relies on an intricate interplay of forces and energy transfer between the skater, wheels, and surface. Biomechanics comes into play as skaters utilize their body's mechanics to generate power, balance, and control while performing various maneuvers. Understanding the biomechanics of balance, stride length, and body positioning can significantly enhance a skater's performance and prevent injuries. Moreover, engineering plays a crucial role in the design and construction of roller skates themselves. Engineers meticulously optimize factors such as wheel size, hardness, bearing type, and boot structure to maximize performance, comfort, and durability. By integrating these principles, roller skating becomes not only a recreational activity but also a captivating exploration of scientific concepts in motion.

Michael Giles
aka Mike Diddy

Facebook: @Mike DiddyGiles | Instagram: @sk8goatofvajit

"Skatetronic"

Also known as Mike Diddy, I hail from Petersburg, Virginia, a small town with a rich history and several notable figures who were born here, including Moses Malone, Blair Underwood, and Trey Songz, among others. Even Martin Luther King Jr. used to visit Petersburg during the Civil Rights era, exerting a significant influence and contributing to the opportunities for freedom we enjoy today. Growing up here, I didn't fully realize how small the town was.

However, I didn't have to venture far to discover my passion: roller skating. I've always had an affinity for anything with wheels that allows for creativity. By creativity, I mean adding your own unique style.

In addition to style, a competitive spirit often comes into play. I'm naturally competitive, and I believe it's a common trait when you're adding style to anything. Without style, one may go unnoticed. Whether you acknowledge it or not, there's a degree of competitiveness in all of us, especially when it comes to seeking recognition from others.

I was raised as an only child by my mother, which drew me more towards sports and hobbies where my performance was the sole determining factor. While I enjoyed the camaraderie of teamwork, I struggled with the frustration of collective punishment for individual mistakes. It may seem contradictory, but that's the reality.

I come from a family deeply rooted in roller skating. Many of my relatives skated during their childhood and continued into adulthood. In the 1980s, when my mother and I lived with my grandma, I recall my older cousins returning from the skating rink with exciting tales of their experiences. They spoke of music, routines, and, of course, girls. Despite being much younger, I eagerly pleaded with them to take me along.

They would just chuckle and reply, "You're too young. Ask your mom to take you to the rink."

Although I had numerous toys, life at the skating rink intrigued me the most. I knew my time would come. In the 1987-1988 school year, rumors spread that the second graders went on a field trip to Rollercade, our local skating rink. Despite never having seen the inside of it, I knew my opportunity was approaching. Finally, in the 1988-1989 school year, when I reached second grade, I got my chance.

Looking back, I realize I was quite an obsessive and detail-oriented child to think about it at such a young age. I didn't join that trip until I was eight in 1989. I saw it as my one shot to prove to my mom that I was serious about going back. When I finally laced up my skates with orange wheels, I did my best despite lacking skill. My determination was high, and I quickly caught on. From that moment on, I was hooked on roller skating, which became a significant part of my life throughout grade school. I was known as the kid who skipped the teen clubs and frequented the skating rink instead.

From childhood to adulthood, roller skating remained a constant in my life. It's where I found my first job, shared my first kiss, met my best friend, and ultimately found my wife, Brandi. Roller skating isn't just a hobby; it's a culture and lifestyle that I've embraced wholeheartedly.

As a pre-teen, I primarily skated in speed skates during the Saturday night sessions at the local rink. I rarely missed a session, except for the occasional Friday night session, which I attended primarily for the races rather than socializing or musical entertainment.

Racing against other kids fueled my competitive spirit, although I wasn't fully aware of it at the time. Winning meant free drinks from the snack bar, a small but meaningful reward for my efforts. This drive to win eventually led me to secure a job at the rink, allowing me to skate for free while on the job.

After high school, I discovered adult skating sessions in Richmond and Smithfield, VA. I, along with my friends, joined the local club in Richmond, which later evolved into Virginia Skate Connection (VSC). The older members welcomed us warmly, nurturing us like their own children. As skating gained popularity in the early 2000s, I found myself traveling to numerous parties and events across different states, further contributing to Virginia's growing skate community.

During this time, social media wasn't as prevalent, and we relied on websites like www.Skategroove.com and www.Jivebiscuit.com for skate news and event updates. It was a period of growth and collaboration, with skaters from different regions coming together to elevate the sport.

My involvement in skating eventually led to opportunities in the film industry. I served as a body double for actor Brandon T. Jackson in the movie "Roll Bounce," an experience that taught me valuable lessons about the business side of entertainment. Despite the challenges, I cherished the experience and encourage aspiring skaters to seize similar opportunities, albeit with caution and foresight.

Now, as I approach forty and embrace roles as a husband and father, skating remains a cherished pastime. I'm grateful for the friendships, memories, and experiences skating has brought into my life. From receiving recognition from Red Bull Energy Drink to finding inspiration in fellow skaters, my journey in roller skating continues to be a source of joy and fulfillment.

Do You Know...

The Purpose of Toe Stops?

Toe stops are essential components positioned at the forefront of roller skates, situated beneath the toe area of the boot. Comprising rubber or plastic materials, they serve multifaceted purposes beyond mere braking. While their primary function involves halting forward motion by pressing them against the ground, toe stops also play a pivotal role in facilitating agile maneuvers and enhancing skater control. By leveraging toe stops strategically, skaters can execute intricate turns, spins, and pivots, leveraging these components as fulcrums to pivot around. Additionally, toe stops contribute to the stability and balance of skaters, providing a reliable point of contact with the skating surface. Their versatility extends beyond traditional skating techniques; advanced skaters adeptly employ toe stops for dynamic maneuvers like jumps and stalls, showcasing the nuanced integration of these components into the skater's repertoire of movements. Thus, toe stops represent not only a means of stopping and steering but also a vital tool for expression and creativity in the art of roller skating.

Lawrence Thomas/ Michael Giles

aka Jit and Diddy

Facebook: @mike.diddygiles | @jit.thomas.1

Instagram: @sk8goatofvajit

"Dynamic Duo"

Hello, fellow skaters! I am Lawrence 'Jit' Thomas, better known as 'Jit,' from the Dynamic Duo alongside my partner, Mike Diddy. Let me take you back to where it all began, around 1996-1997, when we started to take skating more seriously. Our journey in skating commenced during elementary school and continued through high school. We dedicated countless hours to honing our skills, often away from the limelight, until our time in the spotlight arrived. Initially, we weren't exceptional, but with dedication and practice, we saw significant improvement.

Together, we achieved feats we never thought possible. Winning multiple Adrenaline Awards for several consecutive years stands out as our most notable accomplishment. Eventually, the awards committee retired us, declaring that we were ineligible to win any longer. Initially, this felt unjust, but with time, we came to view it as a compliment. With our youthful energy and talent, we represented Virginia proudly, evolving from two young kids into the men we are today. Unfortunately, many new skaters from VA are unaware of our journey, but we urge skaters worldwide to study and understand their history. Today's skating techniques owe much to the legacy passed down to us, particularly from our mentor, Jaye Flynn, who lived in the Tidewater area and influenced our style significantly.

A little about me personally: many may not know that I have a background in dance. I've toured with professional singers and dancers who you might see on TV today. Given my love for music and dance routines, roller skating has always felt like home to me. While I reside in VA, I relocated to Raleigh, NC, where I noticed a different skating style prevalent. People there recognized me, naturally leading to an

interest in learning our style. Hence, many skaters in North Carolina now skate in our distinctive style, which I continue to teach to some extent.

Skating runs deep in both Diddy's and my family. My mother was a skater, and I followed in her footsteps. As a child, I fondly remember playing with her skates on the kitchen floor, which ignited my passion for skating. It's not just a hobby for me; it's part of my identity, as reflected in the skates and laces tattooed on my arm.

Now, let's hear from Diddy.

In the beginning, Jit and I weren't partners. We had another friend with whom we were learning routines. At that time, we hadn't yet embraced the Jammin Technique, so I didn't see the appeal. However, our first visit to Smithfield skating rink in VA for their adult night sparked excitement. Despite being too young to enter initially, Debbie, the rink owner, granted us special permission. Smithfield and other rinks had their star skaters like Cadillac, Junior, and Bryd, while we were just starting out. Our friend eventually left for the military, leaving Jit and me to continue on our own. We leaned on each other for support as we navigated the skating world.

Dwight 'Cadillac' Dodson played a pivotal role in our development. After a falling out in his group, he invited us to join him. Despite being older and more experienced, Cadillac welcomed us and imparted valuable knowledge on music, routines, and even coordinating outfits for out-of-town events. Cadillac's guidance was instrumental in our growth. Years later, both Cadillac and Bryd had the opportunity to be background extras in the film Roll Bounce, shot at Haygood Skating Rink in Virginia Beach by Tyrone Dixon, who also facilitated my role in the film.

Throughout our journey, countless individuals have supported and influenced us at each stage. Though we may not be able to thank everyone personally, we hope this chapter serves as a token of our gratitude. We look forward to seeing you all on the wood, where our passion for skating continues to thrive!

Richard Houston
aka Rockin Richard

Facebook: @Rockin Richard Houston

"Where Do We Go From Here?"

My passion for roller skating started in the late 1950s, and I became obsessed with it. I skated every opportunity I could get out of the house, five or more days each week, with two sessions most days. I wanted to learn everything I could and practice as much as possible. Watching and learning from some of the best senior skaters in the rink, I practiced the moves repeatedly until I mastered them. I had to work on smoothness and showmanship. Every wheel on my skates serves a purpose. When I performed a move and another skater complimented me on it or asked me to do it again or teach it to them, I knew my skating skills were improving.

After working on moves repeatedly, I garnered a lot of attention from other skaters. In the early 1970s, I began entering contests called Be-Bops, which were skating skill contests on the rink floor. The best skaters won trophies for first place, second place, or third place in categories such as Men's Singles, Ladies Singles, and Couples—where men and women skated together. After winning a few Be-Bops, I started getting better at performing on skates. In 1979, while watching the TV show, *The Gong Show*, which featured people doing crazy things, I decided I wanted to skate on the show and win that $500 *Gong Show* Trophy. I called NBC Studios in Hollywood, and they gave me an audition date. Getting there was another thing. Flying was too expensive for me. I got on a Greyhound Bus, and three days later—badly needing a shower—I arrived in Los Angeles, California. I arrived just three hours before my audition time. Friends were waiting for me at the bus station to take me to NBC Studios. After qualifying for the show, nothing was going to stop me from winning. Two weeks later, on

the day of the show, I was a nervous wreck but ready to roll because I knew I couldn't go back to Detroit without that trophy (and the cash).

After Chuck Barris, the show's host, introduced me, the curtain opened, and everyone was watching me. That was another out-of-body experience, and I kept thinking, Feet, don't fail me now.

After winning *The Gong Show* on roller skates in 1979, I returned to The Gong Show stage that same year as a paid guest performer, which excited me greatly. Meeting celebrities at NBC studios who appreciated what I was doing on skates and knowing they also roller skated had me on a cloud that would never fade. Every skater who accomplished something on skates that took them to another level knows what I'm talking about.

In 1985 in Detroit, I opened for James Brown at a fashion show and concert on Woodward Ave and Grand Blvd. You should have seen me modeling on wheels. After the show, as I was walking past James Brown's dressing room and leaving the venue, he called out for me to come into his dressing room.

He said that was one of the best jamming on skates he had seen in a long time, and it looked like I was having fun. First, it took me a few seconds to gather myself. Here was the Godfather of Soul, talking to me and telling me he saw me skating and he was impressed with it.

I said, "I feel alive when I'm skating. Being in control of the wheels also makes you show off with a feeling of I got this."

He said, "Keep doing it until it's not fun anymore. Then, you stop."

That was great motivation for me to keep rolling every chance I could, after hearing that from James Brown, The Godfather of Soul, The Hardest Working Man in Show Business. Something I will remember for the rest of my life. Rest in heaven James Brown.

The Legends in the Sky Skating Party on November 2, 2019, in Washington DC, in a building thirty-one floors up, was a high that took a long time for me to recover. Roller skating on the 31st floor, surrounded by 200, 12-foot-tall glass windows, skaters dressed in formal wear while sipping champagne, eating hors d'oeuvres, and listening to Vaughan Mason sing "Bounce, Rock, Skate, Roll" live made my night perfect. That night was the last time Vaughan Mason performed live for skaters. Vaughan Mason received his skating wings on April 4, 2020. Rest in heaven, Vaughan Mason. Your song will live on forever.

That was the start of the type of skating parties we would present to the world because technology has caught up with our talents. We are in for years to come. We must leave everything we have for the younger skaters following in our footsteps. No matter what city you are from or the type of style you have, we must stay different to learn from one another, to keep new styles forming that will have us skating forever. That's the key to this puzzle of skating. That is how I learned different moves from watching other skaters doing their thing. You take that move and go into your Rolodex of moves that you have in your head and find a place for it, when you hit the wood or whatever surface you're skating on. I can watch skaters perform all day long and come up with a book of moves to learn from. That is why we need each other to pass it down.

Now, let me try to explain what twenty-five-and-over or thirty-and-over old school and new school mean to me. This is just my observation from watching skaters over fifty years old, going in circles, doing things that still amaze me. This means that no matter how many times you go skating, you will see a skater performing something different. Going to skating parties happening all over the country is so much fun to attend. The problem comes when someone asks what is age eighteen and over, or age twenty-five and over. The stated age range tells a skater if they are going to the party or not.

Because of the music, the number one reason for attending the party or not is because of the stated age range. Back in the day, the entire family went skating and listened to the same music. Now, all that has changed. We have rap and hip-hop for the young skaters (new school). Some older skaters also enjoy it. R&B and jazz are for the older skaters (old school). The different music genres make it extremely hard for a DJ to make everyone happy. Older skaters sometimes want to move slower and glide to the smooth beats coming from The Whispers or The O'Jays. Younger skaters want a faster beat to go ninety miles an hour. They need to burn that energy off, and R&B will not cut it.

The skating party hosts should follow the example of Joi in Atlanta. Joi had a thirty-and-over session for the adult skaters from 9 pm to 12 am followed by a 12 am to 5 am session for eighteen or twenty-one and over. The DJ loved her for it. Some thirty-and-over skaters will stay to enjoy skating longer; some will do a meet and greet, shop the vendors, or skate again if they hear a beat they like. Most of all, you will have everyone in the building to share old and new things about skating. Vendors will sell more goods and services related to skating. Older skaters may teach the younger skaters. And the younger skaters, who are serious about becoming better, will listen to what they have to say. Professionals, like doctors, lawyers, police, attend the thirty-and-over skating party.

We don't have time for insecure skaters. You can check that at the door. We don't have time for skaters that can't handle their girlfriend or boyfriend skating with someone or talking to someone, or skaters who want to fight because someone bumped into them by accident. We don't have time for that. It's a grown folks' party. We went to Chicago to a thirty-and-over skating party at the rink from 10 am to 2 pm. Skaters were coming in with suitcases containing ballroom shoes to dance in, cards to play bid whist, chessboards, and ping-pong paddles. These are some things an eighteen-and-over party will not have.

There's a code you must live by to become a thirty-and-over skater. You must know how to talk on our websites, Facebook, and skating shows, among others. Our goal is to pass our talents on to anyone who wants to learn and have fun along the way. With skating, all you have to do is ask. I get a lot of joy when I see someone hitting one of the moves I created (only a real skater is going to understand what I just said).

To all the skaters we have lost because of the COVID-19 pandemic and other causes, my prayers go out to all the families. We have lost some skating styles we will never see again, and that's a shame. We must and will have a tribute for all the skaters that we have lost during this crisis that held us back for over a year from having bigger and better skating parties. We love skating so much that we will skate on anything smooth (indoors or out). The skating coverage from the press during this pandemic is a testament to our love for skating and the thousands of skaters who have joined the movement to catch that thrill on wheels.

We must be smart during this pandemic and wear a mask, wash, and sanitize hands, and maintain social distancing so that we can roll through this setback. It won't be long now. We have come too far to roll back now.

Take this time to think about all the new things we can do, and when the time is right, bring them to life. This is one big party, and if we roll it right, the sky's the limit. Skating has fulfilled so many things in my life. My health is amazing, which is at the top of the list of benefits from skating. My kids—sorry, my grown kids' health is great because they skate as well. One of my sons, Greg, even fastens his skates in a seatbelt in the front seat of his vehicle on his way to the skating rink to keep his skates safe. One of my joys in life is seeing Greg skate and develop a style of his own, as well as watching him skate with different skaters and learning the style of other skaters. He also likes it when we skate together. His eagerness to learn from everyone is helping him become a better skater.

I will end by saying this to every skater: Enjoy the ride. It will pay off in more ways than you can imagine.

Do You Know...

Roller Skating and COVID-19

    Roller skating has experienced significant cultural impacts, notably during the roller disco craze of the 1970s and its resurgence during the COVID-19 pandemic. In the late 1970s, roller discos became social hotspots in the United States, merging disco music with roller skating. This era was characterized by vibrant fashion, rhythmic skating routines, and was immortalized in movies like "Roller Boogie" and "Xanadu," making roller skating an iconic element of the decade's culture.

    The COVID-19 pandemic sparked a renewed interest in roller skating as people sought safe, enjoyable outdoor activities. Social media platforms played a crucial role in this resurgence, with influencers sharing videos that highlighted skating's fun and nostalgic appeal. This revival brought back retro fashion trends and led to increased sales of roller skates. Beyond physical activity, roller skating provided a sense of community and mental health benefits during a challenging time. This renewed popularity continues to influence contemporary culture, demonstrating roller skating's lasting appeal and adaptability.

Myesha McCaskill
aka Smooth Goddess

Facebook: Myesha McCaskill | Instagram: @inspiredbyfavor

"My Skating Journey"

My skating journey has unfolded over the past twenty-eight years. I began skating at the age of ten, with one particular day standing out in my memory: riding on the expressway with my mother, I spotted a skating rink nearby and expressed my desire to skate there. She bought me a pair of rollerblades, and from that moment, the rest became history! Interestingly, many people don't know that I started with rollerblades before eventually switching to quads. When I finally started skating at the rink, I noticed all the other kids had roller skates, and I thought that was the coolest thing! So, I told both of my parents that I wanted roller skates for Christmas. When I finally got my first pair of roller skates, I would go skating every single Saturday in Gurnee, IL. However, my joy was dampened when my mother informed me that we had to move back to Chicago due to her new job. This saddened me greatly as I had formed many connections with the people at the rinks and at my school at that time.

At the age of twelve, I found a new home at The Rink Chicago, where many of my talents began to flourish. It was there that I discovered the JB style of skating, which captivated me. I admired Old School Skate Pioneers such as Duane Hibler and Derrick Lewis, studying their movements and striving to imitate them while grooving in Hyde Skates. Thus began my journey of self-teaching! I learned to develop my own skating style, constantly upgrading my skillset to surpass the competition. From ages ten to twenty-five, I became a cultured self-taught skater. In my twenties, I had the privilege of joining an amazing female skate group called the 'Center of Attention,' led by Paris White. Through this group, I skated with women from Chicago, Florida, and Atlanta. When I turned twenty-five, I began branching

out, learning from mentors such as Josh 'Bat Smoke' Smith, who taught me groundwork; Calvin, who taught me balance, control, and basic spins; and finally, Elon King Eway, who honed my skills in musicality, JB Skate Style, advanced movement, and transitional combinations of moves.

Growing up at The Rink Chicago also provided me with my first job as a skate guard and cashier in the ticket office, thanks to the former rink owners, Carmen and Nate, who gave me this opportunity at the age of 16. I am forever grateful to them for instilling in me the importance of community work in the skate culture, which is why I am so passionate about teaching skating and serving the community. Even when I went away to college, I continued to return on holidays, eager to skate. My first skate jam in 2012, located in North Carolina, exposed me to other skate styles and cultures, enriching my skating experience.

From that moment on, I was determined to become a better skater, diversifying my skills to skate to all types of music and connect with skaters from different cities. I practiced various skate styles, which opened doors and connected me with elite skaters, influencing me to improve my skills and showcase my talents on different platforms.

Though I consider myself primarily a JB skater, I have embraced diverse styles, entering national competitions and featuring in documentaries and television series, such as The Chi. This journey led to the creation of Inspired by Favor, an organization born out of my passion for skating and teaching. Through this platform, I aim to serve the Chicagoland area and inspire others to pursue their dreams.

In conclusion, my skating journey, spanning 28 years, has been guided by hard work, dedication, and the favor of God. Teaching skating classes at Glenwood Roller Rink every Saturday is not just a job but a fulfillment of my purpose. I hope my story empowers others to realize that with God's favor, all things are possible, and with hard work and dedication, dreams can become reality.

James Rich

aka BuckWild

Facebook: James Rich | Instagram: @buckwildjrich

"Becoming BuckWild"

I will never forget that day in 1982. I was walking back from the water after enjoying some nice waves while boogie boarding at Venice Beach with my best friends from high school. In the distance, I heard music playing. Being the music lover that I was, I naturally gravitated towards it. I came around a huge wall, and there they were: the Venice Beach Skaters, skating on a path that led to what was then the Damson Oil Facility. As I got closer, I was amazed.

I had skated before; I played hockey when I was twelve. But I had never seen anything like this. Grown men dancing on roller skates. There was MAD, Terrell, Kyle, Shawn, and several others, who are still close friends of mine to this day, grooving to the latest rap and R&B sounds that I loved. I was mesmerized. All the way home, I couldn't stop talking to my friends about this artistic gift I had witnessed. I wanted to try it, but I didn't have any skates. As the thoughts of what I had seen that day started to fade by night, I was approached by one of my good friends, who had listened to me rant and rave all day about the roller skaters.

Out from behind his back came a pair of blue suede skates with big yellow wheels, yellow laces, and yellow stripes down the side. My eyes lit up.

He said to me, "Try these on. See if they fit."

I couldn't get them on fast enough. They fit me like a glove. It felt like they were meant for me. At that moment, my life changed. I could hardly sleep that night.

When I woke up the next morning, I headed to Venice Beach, excited to see if I still had a tidbit of the skills I had possessed as a hockey skating kid.

I walked up to the skate path, and there they were as if they had never left. These skaters were in their element, grooving to one of my favorite songs, "So Fine" by Howard Johnson. I put on my new brightly colored used skates and stepped out onto the skate floor. Whoop! I hit the deck.

I could have walked away and ended my career before it even got started, but being as determined as I was, I got right back up and took my first baby steps as a Venice Beach Skater. The rest is history.

It took me years to master certain moves that were well respected in the skate world. Sit spins, crazy legs, alphas, and windmills, just to name a few. But my passion truly became choreography. Throughout the years, my friends and I came up with routine after routine. Some, we used for professional shows we performed for thousands of people, and others were just for the spectators at Venice Beach. That was my favorite audience. The people who came from all around the world seemed to live vicariously through us. They would watch us flow on wheels for hours, in amazement, as we freestyled and performed our choreographed hip-hop routines.

Skating has opened many unexpected doors for me, helping me launch several careers. Before I knew it, I was booking gigs. As time went by, I got better and ended up doing commercials for several products, including Pepsi. I also performed in music videos for various artists and all kinds of shows, from corporate events to bar mitzvahs. I would take almost any gig that was willing to pay me for this gift that I had been blessed with. I even ended up modeling for seven years, gracing billboards, magazines, and runways. As a solo skater and as a part of various skating crews, I've blessed stages as an opening act for concerts, done tours teaching people how to skate, and have been able to travel all over the world without spending a dime of my own money.

Eventually, my skate family and I became Venice Beach celebrities. Still to this day, people approach me and tell me how they have been watching us skate for years. Some are inspired to put on skates and join the fun. Others are satisfied by watching us while they hang with friends or have lunch.

One of my favorite projects that I was able to be a part of is the skating documentary Roller Dreams, which tells the history of the

Venice Beach Roller Skaters, and the struggle we've gone through to have our designated skate spot - The Venice Beach Skate Dance Plaza. We went from fighting for a strip of the sidewalk to skate on to having a professionally poured concrete surface made especially for roller skating.

Throughout the years, I've formed amazing relationships with fellow skaters and tourists from all over the world and visited them in their natural habitats and skating rinks. I have so many stories; it's hard to tell them all. From Europe to Asia to Mexico to islands all around the world, I've been able to see different styles of skating that have blown my mind.

My skate style has evolved throughout the years, and I've had many nicknames from Duct-Tape-Jimmy to Organized Confusion to The Skating Tornado, but the one that stuck with me the most was BuckWild. I've received a wide range of comments from people, with some saying that I looked totally out of control, while others were saying that I was one of the wildest skaters they had ever seen. Some thought I looked like I was falling, but I would surprise them by turning the fall into another move, pulling from my large library of moves. I've had people say they thought I was about to hurt myself only to later recognize that it was just my style of skating. It's been said that I flow on skates like water. From a freestyle so smooth that it looked rehearsed to advanced choreographed routines, I was doing what only a handful of skaters could do. That's right! I can keep my ass off the ground and look good doin' it. I have become one of the most versatile skaters around and known by some of the most amazing skaters in the world.

I have been watched by some of the biggest celebrities in the world, but one of my favorite moments was when Debbie Allen, a famous dance choreographer, approached me after watching us skate for a while. She told me that she had done every kind of dance there was. She explained that this was one of the most amazing kinds of dance she had seen and that it was one she was going to leave to us. We both laughed respectfully.

In the last year, skating has exploded. I have been blessed to watch the incredible worldwide surge of new skaters taking to the concrete. For so long, outdoor skating was in decline. It may not have always been apparent, but skating never died. Skating has been alive in rinks all around the world. These rinks have continued to house some of the most amazing skaters in the world, and now that the pandemic has shut down so many rinks, skaters have been forced to skate elsewhere, taking over basketball courts, tennis courts, outdoor hockey rinks, parking lots, and anywhere else they can find a flat smooth surface. This has brought visibility to skating; skaters now have an audience they never could have had before with rink admission fees. Add social media outlets like Facebook, Instagram, and TikTok to the scene; the whole world is now watching roller skaters. Skaters used to be hidden away in rinks or at places like Venice Beach, where you had to see them live and up-close. This phenomenon has been a huge part of the reemergence of roller skating, one of the fastest-growing sports in a long time. Getting a pair of skates has almost become impossible, with incredible wait times for the skates that are out of stock. New skate makers have started to pop up, and seasoned skate companies have had to expand their manufacturing process like they never imagined.

When it was time for me to upgrade from my first pair of brightly colored hand-me-down skates, I turned to skate exclusively in Riedell's. I take skating seriously, and I would only consider the best skating manufacturer for my skates. You wouldn't run a race in flip flops. That's how I feel about my skates.

Blood, sweat, and tears are what I put into my skating. It has kept me young, vibrant, and strong as well as in and out of trouble. Skating is an amazing exercise unlike any other; you work out muscles you don't normally use, and your balance, stamina, and strength are all tested on the skate floor. Trying to keep yourself off the floor is always motivation to get better at this sport. I have torn my medial meniscus as well as wrecked my back, but nothing has stopped me from lacing up. Every time I put on skates, I put my body at risk. I've seen broken bones, compound fractures, busted knees, cracked skulls, knocked out teeth, broken noses, and many other injuries. You would think that would have stopped me from ever putting skates on again, but I'm so addicted to skating that I'm willing to risk my life on the regular. Why? Because when I'm skating, I'm having the time of my life.

To me, music is a gift that has been with me throughout my life, from singing solos in my church choir as a six-year-old, singing opera in college, and becoming a signed hip-hop artist in 1990. Music is the main reason I took to skating so easily. My love for dance has been in my DNA since birth. My love for skating has been with me since I played hockey with my buds as a kid. Put my love for music, my love for dance, and my love for skating together, and you get one of the most skilled dance skaters in the world. After thirty-nine years and over twenty thousand hours of skating, I have put in the hard work to demand respect and to be considered an expert in the field.

No matter what race, religion, or age you are, skating can be for you. It is not prejudiced; it is accepting and non-biased. Skating is something you can do with a crowd of people or something you can do all by yourself. You can compete, or you can do it recreationally. You can get as good as you want through hours of practice, or you can putt-putt around occasionally just to clear your head. It is totally up to you. If you take to it, it is welcoming and challenging. It will test you to your core and make you realize that you are greater than you think. It will push you to be great and stretch your thinking. It will teach you to trust yourself and believe in yourself. When you nail that new move through practice, master a routine, or even choreograph your own, you'll see what you're capable of. Skating is hard. It's strenuous. It's gruesome. It's tough. It's backbreaking and tedious, but if you get good at it, you will have accomplished something amazing.

I encourage anyone and everyone to try skating at least once in their life. It will be one of the most challenging and rewarding things you will have ever tried. For some, it will come easy, and for others, it will be the hardest thing they have ever tried. On some days, I put my skates on, and I'm immediately in a zone. Other days, I put them on, and I can't balance to save my life. Every day is different. Every day is a toss-up. Consistently putting them on can only make the good days outweigh the bad ones.

Skating is my love. It is my all-time favorite activity. I go skating at least two to four days a week. When I'm lonely, I go skating. When I'm full of energy, I go skating. When I want to hang out with close friends or meet new ones, I go skating. When I need to clear my mind of worries, I go skating. I look for every reason to put on my wheels. I look for every reason to choreograph a new routine. I get excited when

I'm going skating. When I am bored with work all week and a skate session is right around the corner, I crave skating like an addictive drug, like a lover I can't wait to see, like my favorite food I can't wait to eat, like the release from an intense workout. It is my serenity, my freedom, my healer, my religion. My escape. My true love. It helps me soar. Skating is life to me.

My love for skating has taught me many things. One of them being that if you do something long enough, you will get good at it. I use this theory in everything I pursue. All aspects of my life have benefited from the hard work and dedication skating has inspired in me. I've gotten my film production degree as well as a culinary certification. I've started successful businesses, worked for companies like Patina Restaurant Group and BET, and worked with celebrities like Shaquille O'Neil, LL Cool J, Cicely Tyson, Babyface, and hundreds more. I'm a licensed Armed Security Guard and Certified Quality Insurance Officer. I now own income-generating real estate and continue to find ways to keep my financial independence, so it is possible to go skating whenever I want. I am grateful for being born in Los Angeles, CA, and to live on Venice Beach because it is such a special place in my heart and has become such an important part of who I am.

I am extremely blessed. Skating will always be an integral part of my life and has done so much for me that now I want to spread the love through teaching. I love teaching choreography from beginning to advanced routines, as well as individual moves. My mission is to teach as many people as I can how to skate and to become legends like myself.

Eric Alston

Facebook: @Eric Alston | Instagram: @ericalston_universalroller

"Skating Success"

I've always skated; I seriously can't remember not skating. I went for the first time on a Sunday, November 13, 1966, to be exact, the day before my fourth birthday, to Empire Rollerdrome in Brooklyn. My mom took me at least once a month until I could go there on my own with my sisters and friends from my neighborhood around the age of ten.

We moved to Queens in May of 1977, and in August of 1978, Saint Albans Roller Rink opened eight blocks from my house. It was a serious trek getting to Brooklyn to skate, and I was elated to have a much closer option. The last Sunday of that month was my first time seeing adults skate because prior to that I had only been to family sessions.

There, I saw a guy named Derrick Williams couple skate with Sally Robinson, and I was instantly hooked. I was determined to learn how to skate like that! I didn't understand the magnitude of the moment, but it was the absolute genesis of my love of skating.

I returned the next night, and I have never been off my skates for longer than two weeks since. I attended every single adult session there for an entire year until they closed for a month to redo the floor after a pipe burst. During that time, I ventured out and proceeded to do what I do today, finding new places to skate, meeting new people, connecting with new energies, and discovering styles, moves, wheels, boots, cities, states, and countries.

I currently reside in Atlanta, which has become the true mecca of our art, because every major style of skating is well represented here. This period has become skate nirvana for me, as we have skating seven days a week and multiple rinks, where we can roll at sessions that are well attended with a live DJ. During the era of Covid, we are one of the

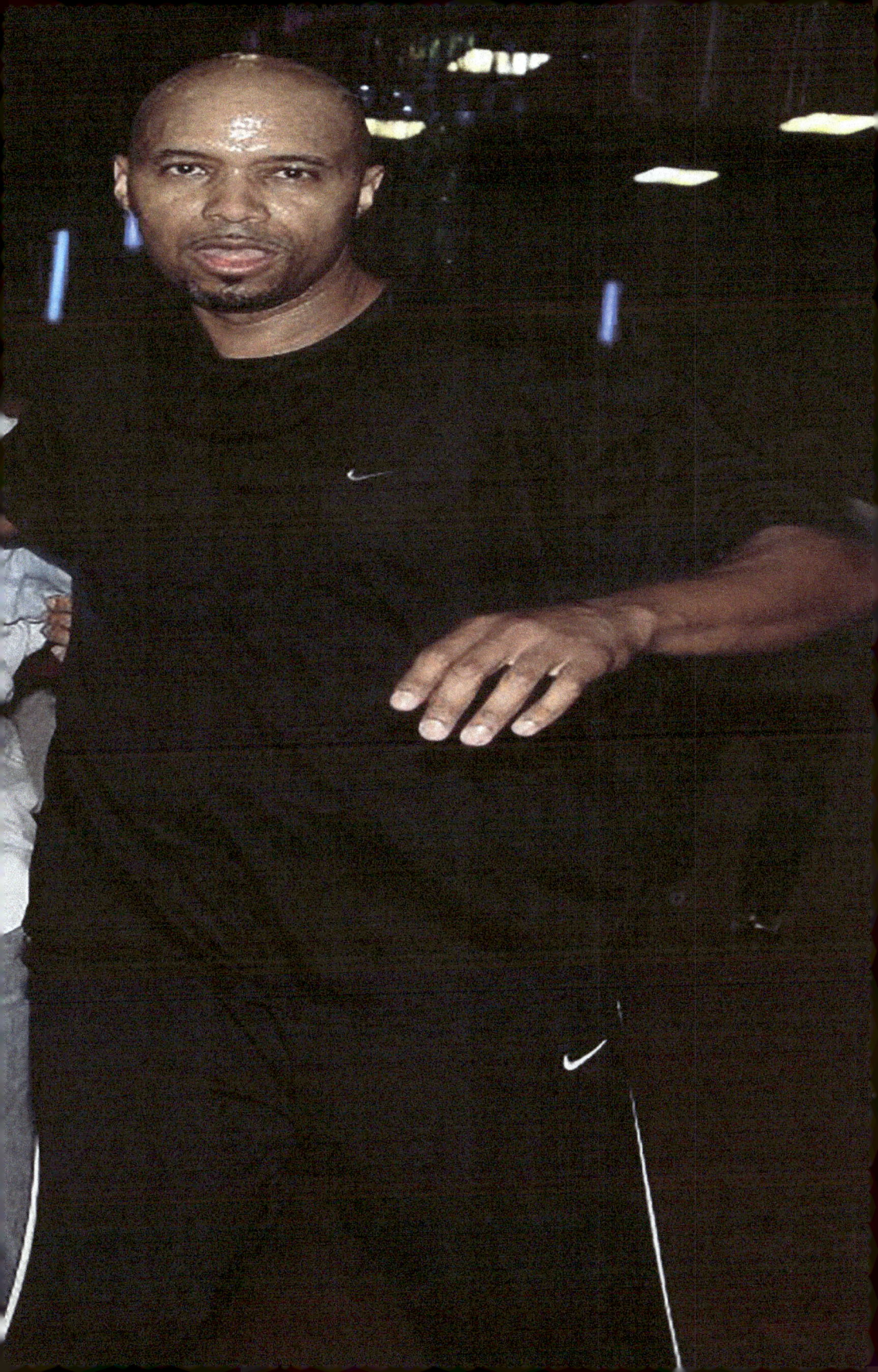

most fortunate areas in the world to be able to engage in our passion virtually unimpeded, and for that, I'm eternally grateful.

I owe skating a debt I can never truly repay. Skating kept me off the streets and out of trouble, it contributes to the great health I've been blessed with, it's given me a respite during some of the most turbulent periods of my life, introduced me to friendships that I've been in all of my adult life, and placed me in contact with some of the most impactful individuals I have ever met.

Skating has allowed me to become a mentor, coach, and trusted confidant to some of the most talented, promising, and enterprising young people within our culture. Success means the progressive realization of a worthy ideal to me. I'm witnessing the evolution of skating. I have contributed to leaving things better than I found them. I feel I have honored our predecessors and those who have poured into me in the process.

Chuck Burch

Facebook: @Chuck Burch | Instagram: @chuckburchcpa

"CPA, Money Man, Influencer, Speaker"

The goal of roller skating isn't about mimicking others, seeking approval, or showcasing skills. For me, it's about carving out my own space, finding my rhythm, and skating at my own pace. As a skater, I'm constantly mindful of my journey and where I aim to go. Roller skating isn't just a pastime; it's a transformative experience that shapes habits, reinforces positive behaviors, and even has the potential to save lives. The skills I develop on wheels extend beyond the rink, becoming second nature and guiding my actions in everyday life. By sharing my passion for skating and encouraging others to join the Sk8 Culture, I'm actively making a difference.

In my story, I share my journey alongside the lessons I've learned and the legacy I'm building through skating. Every day, I serve as a coach, mentor, and problem-solver, helping others achieve their own skating goals. Each moment on the rink presents new challenges and opportunities for growth, providing a sense of stability and tranquility amidst life's uncertainties.

My energy on wheels is palpable, reflecting my passion for the sport. Like many, my journey has been filled with triumphs and setbacks, but I choose to focus on the lessons learned and the goals ahead. While my background growing up in Detroit and navigating through college and entrepreneurship could be seen as obstacles, I prefer to highlight the actions taken to overcome them and thrive. It's through these actions that I've found success, establishing myself as a pioneer in the skate community and shaping my own path in the business world.

I grew up in Detroit, Michigan, in a single-parent home as the oldest of three children. Neither of my parents completed college, and my father left the picture early on. My mother demanded that my

siblings and I, from a very early age, be good students, encouraging us not just to excel academically, but also to engage in athletics. She kept us busy so that we would avoid getting caught up in the perils of Detroit. She modeled an exquisite work ethic and provided love and support every day. We didn't realize what we didn't have. We had love. We were around like-minded people who were going through the same experiences. That was enough for us to get by.

Though my mother and father met at a skating rink, a fact that I did not know until I was a teenager, she made sure that all her children knew how to skate and were "equipped" to skate as well as she did. As a matter of fact, my mother skated well into her sixties. At the age of four, my mother gave me and my brother our first pair of skates. They were metal skates that clipped onto our shoes. They were adjustable in size as long as you kept the skate key that allowed you to tighten and loosen the skates around your shoes. At that time of life, we skated outside, in our basement or anywhere we had space to roll. We skated while playing baseball, football, and even hockey. We had to be creative as we could not leave from in front of the house and had to be home by the time the streetlights came on (someone knows what I am talking about). After nearly wearing out the metal wheels and losing the key often, my mother allowed us to earn the money to purchase our own skates and allowed us to go with her to the skating rink and as a pre-teen, and allowed us to ride the bus to the nearest skating rink, which was the Northland Roller rink.

My aunt and uncle (who were really like our older brother and sister) and older cousins noticed that we would do almost anything to go skating. Thus, many times, allowed us to do their chores in exchange for taking us skating. Between the church skating outings, youth organization skating parties, and the times we could get to the rink for the family session, we created enough opportunities to skate. Though I could never be confused with a rink rat, I could move around the rink with confidence and was athletic enough to win the skate races.

In high school, our family situation moved us out of the city of Detroit to one of the suburbs (Romulus) where my Grandmother lived. There, we did not have as many opportunities to skate (there were no nearby rinks) and as I became active in athletics (basketball, track, and football). Somewhere along the way, someone told me (falsely, of course) that roller skating would have a negative impact on my in-season sports and that I should not compromise athletic promise by roller skating. Thus, I became "too cool" to roller skate. Throughout the early years of high school, I literally stopped roller skating completely, much to the disappointment of my mother.

At that time (high school), my youngest aunt, judicious about her money and how to effectively spend it, encouraged me to start tracking my spending. She pushed me to enroll in a high school bookkeeping course to study finances and learn to take control. I had a giant crush on the teacher (who I learned later in life was a roller skater) and found a new obsession with the power of choice in finances. With little money and no job, I had to become frugal, so as a teen, I knew the importance of the value of money.

My younger cousin's birthday party was coming up, and she wanted to go skating. It had been a couple of years since I had been skating, but I thought it would be a fun way to reconnect with my family and enjoy an activity together. At the rink, I was introduced to the magic of skate dance, and I instantly fell in love. I felt like I was back home, back where I belonged. From that moment on, I knew that roller skating would be a significant part of my life once again.

After that birthday party, I started going to the rink regularly, practicing my moves, and honing my skills. I became obsessed with perfecting my technique and learning new tricks. I attended skate meetups and workshops, soaking up as much knowledge as I could from experienced skaters. Roller skating became not only a hobby but also a passion and a way of life for me.

As I progressed in my skating journey, I felt compelled to share my passion with others. I started teaching skating lessons at the rink, passing on what I had learned to beginners and helping them develop their skills. I also began performing skate routines at events and competitions, showcasing the beauty and artistry of roller skating to wider audiences.

One of the most rewarding aspects of being a skating instructor is seeing my students grow and improve over time. It brings me joy to witness their confidence soar as they master new moves and overcome challenges on the rink. Roller skating has the power to transform lives, and I am grateful to be able to play a part in that transformation for others. In addition to teaching and performing, I have also been actively involved in building and nurturing the roller skating community. I organize skate meetups, events, and social gatherings where skaters of all ages and skill levels can come together to share their love of the sport. These gatherings foster a sense of camaraderie and belonging among participants, creating friendships and memories that last a lifetime.

Through my involvement in the roller skating community, I have met people from all walks of life who share a common bond through skating. Whether we're skating together at the rink or enjoying a meal after a session, the connections I have made with fellow skaters are invaluable to me. Roller skating has not only enriched my life personally but has also given me a sense of purpose and belonging within a supportive and inclusive community.

As I look to the future, I am excited about the possibilities that roller skating holds. I hope to continue spreading the joy of skating to others and inspiring the next generation of skaters. Whether it's through teaching, performing, or community building, I am committed to sharing my passion for roller skating and helping others discover the thrill and fulfillment it can bring to their lives.

In conclusion, roller skating has been a transformative journey for me, shaping who I am as a person and enriching my life in countless ways. From the exhilarating feeling of gliding across the rink to the friendships forged along the way, roller skating has truly been a gift. I am grateful for every moment I get to spend on eight wheels, and I look forward to many more years of skating adventures ahead.

Lynna Davis
aka Lynna Moving Star

Facebook: @Lynna Davis | Instagram: @lynnamovingstar

"My Incredible Skate Love"

Roller Skating has been extremely essential in my life, mentally, physically, spiritually, and financially. It all started in Detroit, Michigan. Being a native Detroiter, roller skating was a prime example of fun, exercise, entertainment, and creativity. It was taboo for us to go to the roller rinks due to the fear that Mom and Dad had for our safety.

"Ma, can we go roller skating at the Arcadia?"

"No," was her answer. "How many times do I need to tell you? They have fought and sometimes people get killed. No, you're not going and don't ask me that question again. Find something else to do."

Well, little did she know that we were sneaking off to the Arcadia Roller Rink. My brother and I would go and be amazed by the skills of the skaters. Most times, we would just stand at the rail and feel the breeze from the locomotive speed of the skaters. We were in absolute awe just watching. When I finally got the nerve to get on the skate floor, blood rushed through my body. I knew that once I became a defensive skater instead of an offensive skater, I would be good.

In the mid-1980s, I moved to New York City to pursue a career in show business. Not only did I study acting and multiple kinds of dancing, I made sure I found time for roller skating.

During this time, no real roller rinks existed in Manhattan. We had small clubs. I remember the Village Skate and Metropales. We had several rinks in Jersey, Laces and many other rinks. I was skating four, maybe five, nights a week. We had a rink in the Bronx named Skate Key. Oh! We turned it out every time we went.

When the Roxy Roller Rink opened, I became an official without a membership. Every Wednesday, my friends and family knew exactly

where I was, Lynna' was at the roller rink. Sometimes, friends would ask if they could go with me.

I would say, "Of course but once I get there, you are on your own because I'll be busy skating. Yes, I'll take you around a few times, but this is my skate night. It's my me time. Time to use my body to its fullest extent. I have to go in to release any stress I might have. Try new things on my wheels. Skate around the rink as many times as I could. Warm my body up."

As soon as I was there, then I knew it was time to go to the middle of the rink and show out and dance on my skates like it was the last party on earth.

Then, I would say, "Oh, please! Please! Play one of my favorite songs. Yeah, the one by James DTrain. Keep on."

The chorus is, "The sky is the limit. So, we just have to keep on keeping on."

I loved hearing Patti Labelle's 'The Rhythm in My Soul'. There's a line in that song she sang, "I can dance upon a dime, give back five cents, keeping time. The one thing you can't take from me is the rhythm I feel deep in my soul."

When daylight came, I was leaving the dance/skate floor. By nighttime, I was back for more. Oh, yes! When the music comes on, skaters get into a zone that only they know about.

Skaters would come up to me and say, "Do that again." I would reply, "What did I do?"

I was so caught up in my skate zone that I didn't always know what I had done. Oh, skating can make you feel so good. You really don't want to stop. The vibe in the skate circles is the most incredible. Sometimes, it depends on what a person is there for.

I wasn't into dating where I skated. I've seen how it caused many problems and could ruin what you came to do. Then, on the flip side, some people found their spouses there. Many of us came to do the same thing: skate and create.

Everyone's having a rocking roll jamming good time.

While skating at the Roxy Roller Rink, I was with the Emperor Clothing Designer, Ellie Tahari, the Magnificent Bill Jamming Butler, Actor Khalil Kain and a host of celebrities. My skating skills took me to

Japan to open for a brand, 'Peace, Love, and Happiness', a fashion show in Mexico. It allowed me to perform the 'Half-time show of the New York Knicks, Trolls Movie Promo Choreographer, and Casting. The Avicii made me official, giving me the title of choreographed casting director and consultant. My skating skills also took me to ABC Localish Casting; The Big Celebrity Fundraiser Robinhood Foundation, Cynthia Rowley Fashion week, Targets XXO ANNIVERSARY, the launch of a Corporate Celebrity Designer party, Former Ladies of Chic Skating trio, NYC Roadrunners skate show at the finish line, Featured Skater Show Lost in the Disco.

When you find your passion, God will make sure you get paid.

SKATE 2 FAME Helpful Hints
- Skating is not a competition, it's an expression of skills, style, and creativity.
- If a skater or anyone ever tells you to stay in your lane, just say, "That's Lame. God blessed me not only with the highway, I'm also blessed with the skyway. Amen. God has blessed us all with many talents. In my house, there are many mansions. If not, I wouldn't have told you so."
- Never take credit from another skater and try to make it yours. Just because you change the music or eliminate other talent does not make it your property, just for social media fame. NOT GOOD.
- Most successful people work hard to get where they are. I know it may look like an overnight success. No, it takes many hours, days, and years to arrive there.
- Be sincere about what you want from another person. This will allow you to have a wonderful relationship with yourself and others.
- Most times, it is not just about your talent. It's also about your integrity and honesty. Respect for others and self-respect will take you a long way.

Do You Know...

Rollin' in the ATL!

Roller skating became especially popular in Atlanta, Georgia, due to a unique blend of cultural, social, and historical factors that fostered a vibrant skating scene.

Atlanta has a rich musical heritage, particularly in hip-hop and R&B, which played a significant role in popularizing roller skating. Many roller rinks in Atlanta embraced these genres, hosting skate nights featuring live DJs and music that resonated with the local community. This connection to music made skating an appealing activity for many young people.

The roller skating community in Atlanta is known for its inclusivity and strong sense of camaraderie. Skaters of all ages, backgrounds, and skill levels come together at local rinks, fostering a welcoming and supportive environment. This sense of community has helped sustain the popularity of roller skating in the area.

Atlanta has several well-established roller rinks that have been central to the local skating scene for decades. These venues, like Cascade Family Skating and Golden Glide, have become cultural landmarks where generations of Atlantans have skated, socialized, and enjoyed music.

Roller rinks in Atlanta serve as important social hubs, especially for African American communities. They provide a safe and enjoyable space for socializing, celebrating events, and participating in community activities. This social aspect has been crucial in maintaining the popularity of roller skating.

The portrayal of roller skating in popular media has also boosted its appeal. The 2006 movie "ATL," which features prominent scenes in a roller rink, highlighted Atlanta's skating culture and brought it to a wider audience. Such representations have helped cement roller skating as a significant part of Atlanta's cultural identity.

Tony Sailor
aka Sick on Skates

Facebook: @Tony Sailor | Instagram: @sickonskatescrew

"Atlanta Passing the Skate Torch"

To break down the ATL Skate Style, you must understand the history of Atlanta Culture. The language, attire, music, and beliefs all affect how we skate. Think of a family of seven, mother and father, who married and produced five children. Understand that the style was created because of the black household. Therefore, the moves are related in some form or fashion, sharing unique sequences and swag. Those interested in learning the style must trust the process.

The Style can be described by visualizing aggressive but coordinated movements, which mirror the cadence of a song. These are created in forms of a drum major, step master, or choir. When you bring the same to skates, you will discover that movements, mostly, are done in unison. If you're raised in the South, you can identify with the musical tunes that rattle the streets of Atlanta—gospel or hip hop.

This gives birth to certain iconic dances that originated and evolved from this region. The move called "The Skate" is still in practice and taught on and off skates. It has become universal to each era in Atlanta. It is demonstrated in the skating routine called "The Stab." It was a normal movement in the Yeek Style of the dance routine called "The Devastator." The connection between skating and dancing goes hand-in-hand in Atlanta. Music can alter how we feel and, when combined with skating and dancing, it comes out to express what is being played. For it to make the list under ATL style, however, it must fall under certain criteria to be acknowledged. That is another subject for a different occasion.

Social media has played a role in delivering our content by influencing others to create something similar. Skating evolves as we grow in life. It's fun and entertaining at the same time. Many of us stay connected because of this activity we share, which becomes even more interesting when we can showcase our skills to one another. We relied on one another and

focused on learning as much as possible. We couldn't force our skills and talent. We could only do what was normal at the time: trust the process.

The more authentic the song is to the region, the better it is to understand the expression of the movement by the inhabitant of the area. Since we may have been born in different eras, the era determines the movement that would become catchy to the masses in that region. This movement would become popular and develop a name.

For example, "Seeking" or "Yeek" is a popular style developed in Atlanta that began in the early 80's. A group of individuals formed a crew called "FDC" or Fresh Dancing Crew. The style they created evolved to many movements and routines that branched out to those who could skate. Most of the known iconic dance battles and music performances took place in skating rinks. This became a tradition that was passed from generation to generation. And like any era, evolution took place.

ATL Skate style has many known forms of movement. The Stab, The Prep, Bounce, and Ryde can all be linked back to Yeeking. Sick on Skates Crew, a group of talented skaters have continually demonstrated the ATL skate style and incorporated new variations with each generation.

There have been many older individuals, who taught and mentored the style. They include Vaughn Newton, Anthony Francis, Levy Johnson, DeAngelo Holt, Breeze Goodman, Keith Donaldson, and AL Fleming "ATL Skate Man." These men are the OGs or the architects of ATL Skate Style. And throughout my life, I have been fortunate to learn from them all.

I was born and raised in Los Angeles, California. I began skating at the age of three. My parents split just before I turned five. When I visited my father in Atlanta, Georgia, the seed was planted when my father brought me to "Jellybeans." This rink is a place where the style was groomed and created. At the age of thirteen, my mother decided to return to Atlanta, and from there, skating found a place with me, yet again.

Once I turned seventeen, I was already mingling with the OGs, trying to learn and keep up. At nineteen, I became a member of skate crews at local rinks such as Golden Glide. I later formed Georgia Rampage or "GRP" skate crew in 2005. The idea behind the birth was to show others in the city and communities the essence of a co-ed local skate crew.

During the years of growing, the awareness of our style and having many successes along the way, I was called to serve my country for the second time. Thus, the team was left in the care of those I hoped understood the logic behind the crew's mindset. Unfortunately, upon my return, the crew suffered compromising issues leading to financial and toxic leadership. This situation, which led to the dismissal of members, forced me to permanently dissolve GRP INC. Nonetheless, rogue individuals persisted and continued to operate GRP, but eventually succumbed to its downfall. Luckily, the passion and desire I had for skating still existed; thus, in 2009, the creation of Sick on Skates Crew came to be.

This time, I wanted to go deeper into the history of where the ATL style originated. I removed myself from what I learned from rink peers and searched out those from that past. Throughout my search, I was joined by like-minded individuals such as Corey Bing, who helped maintain structure and balance within the crew. In 2016, SOS was able to link and connect to the founding fathers of the ATL style, who gave guidance on the origin and took the time out to teach us the basics of the style.

This allowed us to adopt the old and combine it with the new. SOS became relevant within surrounding communities and the younger generation by incorporating the style in areas that have nothing to do with skating. This effort benefited from the desire of families and friends to become involved in a growing and existing movement. The crew's efforts have also made a staple in different cities around the United States and have even touched other countries.

As we continue to learn increasingly about the history, we understand how the current generation develops their interpretation of the style. SOS is the first but has been replicated with few tweaks. SOS development has led to teaching and mentoring the youth.

In 2020, SOS produced Kidz Sick on Skate's crew, which focuses on mentoring children and families. Reconnecting the families wishing to skate with each other is a joy and gift at the same time. Skating is an activity many of us enjoy doing together. It is the cohesion that we share amongst our skate mates. Luckily for us, we can pass the torch for others to build and learn from.

Now, things are starting to make sense and, for some of us, passing the torch has been a major achievement. Things have come full circle and what we like to pass along to all interested in our style: just trust the process.

Do You Know...

Roller Skatin' Prez—is it Possible?

Theodore Roosevelt, the 26th President of the United States, was well-known for his vigorous lifestyle and enthusiasm for physical activities. Serving as president from 1901 to 1909, Roosevelt was a proponent of what he called "the strenuous life," advocating for robust physical exercise and an active lifestyle as essential components of personal and national vitality.

During Roosevelt's presidency, roller skating was experiencing a surge in popularity in the United States. The introduction of the modern quad skate in the 1860s had made roller skating more accessible and enjoyable, leading to the establishment of roller rinks in many cities by the early 20th century.

Although there is no definitive documentation or widely recognized historical record explicitly stating that Roosevelt roller skated, it fits well within the context of his adventurous and experimental nature. Roosevelt's known willingness to try new and popular activities of his time lends credibility to the idea that he could have donned a pair of roller skates.

Roosevelt's presidency was marked by his efforts to promote physical fitness among Americans. He supported initiatives like the creation of playgrounds and encouraged physical education in schools. Roller skating, as a burgeoning recreational activity, would have been aligned with his efforts to endorse a physically active lifestyle.

Roosevelt's influence on American culture extended beyond politics. His participation in various sports and activities often inspired the public to follow suit. If Roosevelt had indeed taken up roller skating, it likely would have further popularized the activity.

Doug Mike
aka Sk8 Vidzz

Facebook: @Doug Mike | Instagram: @sk8_vidzz

"The Origin of Sk8 Vidzz"

In 2009, I resumed roller skating after a twenty-plus year hiatus. I used to attend a local session in Macon, Georgia, on Saturdays with my family, including my two daughters and my wife. We would go for a couple of hours and just enjoy ourselves, aiming to make it a weekly tradition. Eventually, I met some regular guys my age who encouraged me to join the adult session on Sunday night.

I attended the adult session and immediately thought, "Yeah, I love this. Let's do it." I kept attending, started learning routines, and had fun with them. Eventually, I got hooked on a style of skating called JB, which is widely known in Chicago. I became fascinated by some of the moves.

We had a skater in our group who knew this style, despite not being from Chicago. He had learned it from Chicago skaters during his visits there and brought the style to Atlanta. Intrigued, I began searching for JB skating on YouTube, learning the moves by watching videos. Eventually, I started going to Atlanta with the guys, planning trips to Golden Glide Roller Rink. I was amazed by the talent and skill level of the skaters there, witnessing various styles and genres of music different from our local session in Macon.

During one of these trips, I recorded some skaters with my cell phone, marking the beginning of my journey in capturing skate videos and the birth of Skate Vidzz. I began searching for roller skating videos online and learned about an event called Skate-a-Thon, where people skate in Atlanta from midnight until 6 a.m. during Labor Day weekend. Intrigued, I decided to check it out with my wife.

Finding parking was a challenge, but once inside, we were amazed by the massive crowd—around one thousand two hundred to one

thousand five hundred people—skating on the floor simultaneously. My wife, a beginner skater, was awestruck and chose to watch while I ventured off to skate and record footage.

The energy and camaraderie at the event were electrifying. Witnessing the roll call, a tradition I had never seen in person, left me in a state of awe. This experience marked the beginning of my journey in capturing skaters on film and eventually led to the creation of Skate Vidzz.

As I began reaching out to skaters and befriending them, I realized the impact I could have by showcasing their talent through my videos. Though I initially faced challenges, such as losing my Skate Vidzz page on Facebook, I persevered, driven by my passion for roller skating and the desire to share it with others.

Roller skating is not just a hobby; it's a passion and lifestyle for many. I wanted to expose others to the vibrant roller skating culture and the dedication skaters invest in their craft. From local sessions to national skate parties, I captured the essence of roller skating and shared it with the world through Skate Vidzz.

Reflecting on my journey as a skate videographer, I take pride in pioneering new techniques and inspiring the next generation of videographers. Though I may not have sought monetary compensation for my efforts, the joy and fulfillment I've gained from documenting the roller skating community have been invaluable.

As I continue to post daily skate videos and contribute to the roller skating community, I hope to inspire others to embrace roller skating as a form of expression, exercise, and enjoyment. Roller skating transcends individuality, bringing people together from all walks of life, and I'm grateful to be a part of this vibrant and inclusive community.

Berri Blanco
aka Straberry Perez

Facebook: @Berri Blanco Perez | Instagram: @thesk8socialite

"I Am the Greatest"

A star was born. I am Berri Blanco, also known as Strawberry Perez! I was born and raised in New York City, The Bronx, the home of HipHop and "FLYizm." Growing up in New York was the best. The music, culture, fashion, and, of course, roller skating.

In August 1980, at twelve years old, my mother took me to a building off of twenty-third street in Manhattan. Downstairs, there was a lounge, but upstairs… "MAGIC." As a punishment, she told me to go upstairs until she finished up with her friends. I walked upstairs towards my punishment, but all I could say was, "WOW!"

The music, the ambiance, the roller skates. It was the best punishment ever! I always tried to get in trouble so she could take me back there. Once she saw how much fun I was having, she switched tactics. I kept roller skating from that day on.

Throughout my years, circumstances and situations led me down different paths. Nevertheless, my heart was always at the "rink." I'm just starting to realize that when you disconnect from your true self and your bliss, you will endure hardship, pain, and suffering, but it can be short-lived. The process is to get back on course and live out your dream.

In May 2015, I moved to Atlanta. As soon as I arrived, I was graced by the presence of the one and only Mr. Bill Butler. You think PRINCE has an aura… Mr. Bill Butler's talks, skating, overall presence are from another world. I started to attend his class. I didn't fully understand his "Jammin" technique, so practicing was essential because I knew this was something great. I was learning, and I wanted to be the best! And I was right!

One night, at an event, a guy walked up to me with his phone in hand and said: "Hello. This is you on my phone and my website. I

am the president of Skatesus, and I would like to sponsor you! Call me!" Yes! I am a National Sponsored Roller Skater with Edea Skates, Rolling & Skates! Still to this day.

Fast forward to the present. The year 2020, I was interviewed by the lovely and spiritual delight, Amirah Palmer. Jokingly, I suggested to her she needs some "Skate Entertainment" on her Podcast. Shortly after the interview, we talked and shared a few ideas. One idea turned us into skate conglomerates, creating skate apparel, writing books, hosting events, and the list continues.

I went from skating as a child to moving to Atlanta where I learned roller skating from the best. Now I have sponsorships, teach skate classes (Skate Finesse), own a skate clothing line (Juci Fruit), have performed at the biggest and best roller skating events to date. Recently, I've been a guest on the #1 Roller Skate podcast (Sk8rz Konnect!).

Now, the expansion of Berri Blanco Entertainment is here! I've truly woken up. My life inspires me every day. And I feel so honored to be in the skate world where I can use my voice and do all the skate greatness I do. Stay tuned! The expansion of STRAWBERRY PEREZ continues.

Eugene White
aka Quad1

Facebook: @Leo White| Instagram: @quad1evolution

"Visions of the One Wheel Roller 'The Inner Life of Leo White'"

I never envisioned that a gift from God could be so powerful and life changing. As a young boy growing up in Missouri roller skating was just a leisurely pastime my family enjoyed every weekend. I recall conversations with my Father, talking about the ownership of our skating rink and the visions of bringing families and people together in unity from a small concept called roller skating.

I was introduced to the sport of skating at the age of six. Our family would skate so often it became my thriving passion to become the best on the hardwood. Skating created an avenue of escapism for me, a place where I could lace up and leave all my troubles and cares of the world on the wood as I dreamt of one day being a legend in the game. As I grew older and continued to perfect my skating style, I was introduced to "Free Style" skating through the mentorship of Bryant Morris, the first person to ever take off the back truck and wheels, mastering a unique competitive style without damaging the hardwood floors. This style intrigued me so much I became a sponge, mentally and physically mastering the techniques in pursuit of creating a style of my own.

While Bryant Morris is the first mentor in a line many, it's legends such as Lisa Boyd, Harpo, Kenny, Kevin Hollywood Brown, Wayne-O, Thomas Bouie and Adrienne, Joe Hill, and Big George (RIP), that I've taken pieces of each one to bring full circle the creation of my brand. After competing successfully in numerous competitions, I prayed for a style that would place me above the ordinary and set me apart from all that brace the hardwood. That prayer was answered in 1997, when I was blessed with perfecting the style of "The One Wheel Roller." This unorthodox style of skating allows me to skate using only one

left front outer wheel on the left skate boot and one right front inner wheel on the right skate boot. To date, there is no skater domestically or internationally capable of skating my perfected style.

The journey of the "One Wheel Roller" hasn't always been smooth sailing. To become a perfected brand, one must endure many trials, tribulations, and sacrifices that will test the very fabric of your soul. Many a night on my knees, I've prayed for wisdom, knowledge, and humility, to move me beyond situations of adversity. Early in my career, I was homeless, hungry, and working for below minimum wage in Atlanta, Georgia to maintain the basic means of survival while pursuing my dream of becoming a skating legend. You see, it takes everyday struggles and sacrifices to build the character and integrity needed to successfully create and manage a business/brand. Knowing what it feels like at the bottom of the game strengthens my inner being to stay mentally focused in my pursuits regardless of the past or present circumstances. To conquer the mental fire within, you must learn how to tame it, not become a slave to it. The public will never understand your fire if they can't visually comprehend how you've moved beyond your trials, unsinged by their very flame.

With knowledge of survival in my veins, I decided in 2001 to aggressively perfect "Leo White", the brand as a dominating presence in the skate community. I started networking my name and skating style to businesses, capturing the eyes of some very prominent organizations to secure roles in commercials, documentaries, and movies as the "The One Wheel Roller."

Becoming well known in the urban skate arena has taught me it takes more than name recognition to build a brand, and how you present yourself to a public audience can make or break the success of your business. With this understanding, I've sharpened my tools in the business and created a brand that is now nationally and internationally known in the skating circuit.

Business is not only about branding. It's about using your influence, knowledge, and connections to further strengthen the community, public outreach, policies, and education that continue the advancement of individuals young and old in their professional pursuits. I've created a business model that will give back to our communities through mentorships, workshops, educational forums, and instructional videos and platforms. Leo's Quad One Evolution International, LLC, is an organization focused on excellence in Black Business.

As the first Black-owned skate manufacturing organization we plan to break down barriers once untouchable in the sports arena. Within my business framework, I've perfected the rollout of signature skate products, and skate apparel through our trademarked "LQ1" brand. Our organization has a strong media presence. We are also leveraging our presence on social media platforms including Facebook, Instagram, and YouTube. Our skate family, and new skate members can follow and view tutorial videos and follow me across the country as I check in with other skate venues and legends throughout the United States and abroad.

In my quiet hours, I find myself extremely humbled by the magnitude of responsibility and success God has blessed me with. It's amazing how a small prayer from a young man in pursuit of a dream can create such profound beauty that can touch so many lives. I'm blessed that roller skating is not only my passion but is now the life's blood that fuels a movement.

With an appreciation for the entrepreneurial process, no job has ever been too messy or difficult to tackle. My hands-on experience assisting in the growth of many existing franchise organizations allows me to perfect my knowledge of the business industry and arms me with a fresh perspective and focus of how to integrate my passion in building a successful business blueprint that other entrepreneurs can glean from in their individual business pursuits.

This journey continues to teach me. I'm forever a student in pursuit of perfection. If I can leave anything through my legacy, I want to impart three profound things I've learned:

First, no matter what obstacles are present in your life, never allow them to deter you from focusing on your dream. We are all given gifts from God to perfect and share with others, and we must endure the trials, tribulations, and growing pains, to ultimately manifest our gifts to the world.

Second, stay grounded. Having a strong spiritual relationship is key to success. As you climb the ladder of success in pursuing your dream, there will without a doubt be people, places, and situations used to detour you from your goals. Don't allow the external noise to drown the voice in pursuit of excellence. Mental and physical focus is key and with the unconditional love of God, all things are possible.

Lastly, I will say enjoy your dream. Have fun, embrace the joy and fulfillment of knowing you are successfully living your passion. It's a beautiful thing waking up each day knowing your life isn't about showing up for a job, because now your passion is your job. A profession I will gladly show up for any and every day of the week.

I hope that the legacy of the "One Wheel Roller" will give back to the world and those fortunate enough to know the brand of "Leo White" will gleam from my presence and the impact of excellence our business represents nationally and internationally.

(Story written by Stacey Kannon.)

Okurut George
aka B-Boy Skater George

Facebook: @george.okurut | Instagram: @okurutgeorge

"Skating in the Motherland"

My journey as a skater started in 2012, when I bought the skate shoe, known as rollerblades from a friend who was selling them for ten dollars.
After buying the rollerblades, I had to teach myself because I didn't have anybody to teach me. My sister never wanted me to learn skating because skaters had a bad image in the country (they were mostly known as thieves). I still wanted to learn. I had been in love and was passionate about skating.

We have bad roads in Uganda, especially in the villages. I always had to hold on to the back of a motorcycle, which would pull me through.

Skating was also something new in Northern Uganda. I remember in 2013, when I went with my skating board to school, all my schoolmates and the villagers would follow me. The Principal had to seize my skateboard because he wanted me to concentrate on studies. He told me I would get it back in 2014 after the final exams. I felt so bad, but I had to obey the rules of the school.

When I was done with school, I went to the city, where I bought new rollerblades. Then, I joined the Uganda Rollball team because I was so passionate about skating seriously and wanted to be someone great, who can inspire and motivate the young generation.

From there, I joined Supersonic Skating Academy, which had programs that taught skating at International School. I worked with them for few months to make money, but I had to go back to into construction, which was my profession.

I really wanted to get serious about skating. I faced several challenges. Skating equipment and shipping was expensive. I couldn't

afford to pay for any of those with my meager salary. Yet, I couldn't get my mind off of skating. I skated for fun but couldn't go all in because we didn't have any good skating parks.

The government doesn't support skating, even though we have a sports council in our country. They don't care about skating, which has discouraged a lot of people from skating. I would love to continue, but I will need more support in building skate parks in different regions of the country. I would love to be a genuine supplier of skating equipment because that's another big challenge.

For now, I'm teaching yoga and acroyoga to different communities because I'm certified to that. I see skating as a way to bring progress in this country. I am looking forward to overcoming the numerous challenges in front of us. With the equipment I will be able to teach more communities.

At this point, I believe that if we, as skaters around the world, come out to support one another, then we shall have a great community of skaters with a great supporting platform for the young generation in different countries.

I am excited about us coming together to make skating great in more African countries.

In Memoriam

"Gone But Not Forgotten"

"Death is not the greatest loss in life. The greatest loss is what dies inside us while we live."
—Norman Cousins

Sending peace and prayers to those in the skate world whom we have lost but who shall never be forgotten:

Anthony (Tex) Smith
Charles (The Wood) Haywood
Linda (Lady Linda) Corley
Will (Mean Will) Reed
CD Man
Scott (Slo Mo) Randolph
Gary (Uncle Peaks) Pete
Morris (Philly Plash) Armstrong
Puerto Rican Mike
Pops
Lakiesha (RedBone) Jones
Jarel (Mello) Joes CCP

DJ DC
Keon Nesbitt CCP
Will Nesbitt
Lezly Ziering
Davie (Brooksie) Allen
Monique (Skate Vixen)
Williams Allen Jetter
Duvall J Stowers
Ever Ready
Yancie Brinkley

For those not mentioned, you will forever be in our hearts, prayers, and with each roll of our wheels.

In Memoriam

A Tribute to Yancie Brinkley...
A Detroit-style Skater

By Patreze Brinkley

Yancie Brinkley, born February 22, 1945, was a Detroit-style skate instructor based in Detroit, Michigan. He began roller skating in 1975 at The Arena skating rink on Greenfield at Grandriver before moving on to Wheels on 8 Mile and Meyers. He ended up at Detroit Roller Wheels, where he taught Advanced Detroit Style roller skating. Yancie participated in and won many competitions with his skate partner, Darryl Thomas, in the late 1970s and early 1980s.

In 1985, Yancie started The Five Star Skate Club, a group of women skaters who performed different themed shows to Motown's greatest hits with him. They earned patches for their skate club jackets from the National Roller Skating Association by entering exhibitions. He also taught his daughter, Patreze Brinkley, to skate as soon as she could stand on them. He made her take classes on the same days he taught classes so she would understand each part of the style from the basics. When she was ready, he introduced Patreze to performing. Yancie did a Popeye the Sailor performance where Patreze was Sweet Pea. This opportunity sparked her inner love for performing.

Roller skating was such a special part of his life, which is why he took it very seriously. He once taught a class about how to care for their skates and what tools to always have in their skate bag. His passion for the technique of the style had led to many becoming talented skaters who are still rolling now. So smooth and precise, people knew him for the way he could slide from the far end to the other side of the floor. He had a mean "step slide," and his "one-foot" and "jump slide" were like none other. Yancie will always be remembered as a pioneer of the Detroit style because of his hard work, skate lessons, theatrical performances, and love for his skate family.

The Five Star began a show for him when he was first diagnosed with cancer in early 1991, and they kept this tribute show going after his passing throughout his daughter's high school years. They raised money for Patreze to help her mother care for her as she was just eleven years old when he died. The skate community stepped up in Patreze's life, so when she returned to skating in 2019, she started his tribute show again to honor The Five Stars.

Every February, in Yancie's honor, Patreze produces a "Detroit Style" performance show, recreating some of the past performances and honoring skaters from the 1970s through the 1990s. If you want to learn more about Yancie and so many other Detroit-style pioneers, watch out for the "Yancie Brinkley Tribute" every February around his birthday.

Amirah Palmer

Facebook: @Amirah Palmer | Instagram: @itsamirahpalmer

"About the Lead Author"

Amirah Palmer is not just a skater; she is a visionary, serial entrepreneur, and the founder and CEO of Sk8rz Konnect. Her platform, Sk8rz Konnect, serves as a showcase for the diverse skills and artistry found in various forms of skating, including roller, ice, and skateboarding. Amirah is a decorated U.S. Army Veteran, an International Best Selling Author, and a graduate of the University of Maryland. Her passion extends to volunteering and community service.

Through The Evolution of Skating series, Amirah Palmer aims to create a unified platform that brings together every genre of the skating arts. Her goal is to connect, showcase, and inspire skaters in their respective fields, fostering a sense of community and encouragement within the skating world.

www.ingramcontent.com/pod-product-compliance
Lightning Source LLC
Chambersburg PA
CBHW050648160426
43194CB00010B/1850